PRAISE FOR *MULTI-ASSET STRATEGIES: THE FUTURE OF INVESTMENT MANAGEMENT*

"The investment industry has historically mostly focused on security selection decisions, a focus that has come as a distraction with respect to another key source of added value, namely asset allocation decisions. In the face of recent crises, and given the intrinsic difficulty of delivering added value through security selection decisions alone, the relevance of the old paradigm has been questioned with heightened intensity, and the focus is shifting towards the proper management of factor exposures as the main source of performance. As part of this developing trend, multi-asset investment solutions have become increasingly popular amongst sophisticated institutional investors focusing on efficient harvesting of risk premia across and within asset classes. In this context, the book appropriately titled *Multi-Asset Strategies: The Future of Investment Management*, edited by Larry Cao, is a timely and welcome initiative. Written in a highly accessible manner and targeting investment professionals with no or little prior exposure to the subject, this text provides a collection of meaningful articles on multi-asset products and solutions. Most interestingly perhaps, it also includes in-depth coverage of examples of implementation from an investor standpoint. This book will prove useful reading for asset owners and asset managers alike."

Lionel Martellini
Director, EDHEC Risk Institute
Professor of Finance, EDHEC Business School

"*Multi-Asset Strategies* is an easy-to-read yet authoritative and up-to-date guide to some of the leading concepts and controversies in the investment industry. Larry Cao acts as editor, setting the themes, selecting well-known experts to write the chapters, and then providing practical applications. Among other issues, the book critically examines asset classes versus factor exposures, dynamic asset allocation, risk parity, and style boxes. Then, case studies provide an inside look at how portfolios are actually managed at three leading global management firms. Although we agree to disagree on some issues, I do recommend this very well-done book."

Roger Ibbotson
Professor, Yale School of Management
Chairman, Zebra Capital Management, LLC

"No one can beat the market all the time. Multi-asset strategies provide an instrument that satisfies the need for asset allocation by all investors, particularly long-term investors. This is precisely where the fundamental value-add of investment managers comes in. *Multi-Asset Strategies: The Future of Investment Management* examines the overall theory and practices of multi-asset investing, providing investment managers with an invaluable reference."

Hong Lei
Chairman, Asset Management Association of China

"Larry Cao has brought together top-flight investment professionals with a diverse approach to multi-asset class management. As a global asset allocator, I very much appreciate the mosaic approach of *Multi-Asset Strategies*. Without doubt, this book leaves the reader with a holistic view of best practice in the field."

Robert Browne, CFA
CIO, Northern Trust

"In theory, multi-asset investing sounds straightforward—invest across a range of diversifying asset classes to generate a long-term return that meets the investor's needs. In practice, it is not as easy as it sounds, integrating a wide range of very different skills across asset allocation and stock selection, as well as requiring deep market knowledge to create carefully structured portfolios that meet investment objectives. The CFA Institute publication *Multi-Asset Strategies: The Future of Investment Management* expertly outlines both the theoretical and the practical essence of multi-asset investing. The case studies and interviews, in particular, provide a deep insight into the practical issues to be considered in making multi-asset investing a success."

Phil Graham, CFA
Deputy Chief Investment Officer, Pacific
Mercer

"I read the book immediately and found it both reassuring and illuminating. It is a thorough review that will be of value to experienced practitioners as well as others who are new to the concepts that underpin successful multi-asset investing."

Martin Atkin
Managing Director, Multi-Asset Solutions Group
AllianceBernstein

CFA Institute

MULTI-ASSET STRATEGIES

The Future of Investment Management

Edited by Larry Cao, CFA

ISBN 978-1-942713-52-4

January 2018

DEDICATION

In memory of Franco Modigliani, who showed me the essence of the research process

PREFACE

At CFA Institute, we take to heart our responsibility to identify industry trends that affect the careers of our members. It is our job to help members stay up to date and to provide opportunities for continuing professional development. One such trend that we have witnessed in recent years is multi-asset investing.

The popularity of multi-asset investing arises from investors' demand for investment outcomes rather than relative performance. Outcome-oriented investing, as it is known, shifts the investment professionals' focus from beating the benchmark every quarter to serving investors' needs. Multi-asset strategies are not only aligned with outcome-oriented thinking but also provide the investment product and solution best suited to the purpose.

One reason that multi-asset strategies have not yet been embraced by the entire investment profession is the myth that the asset allocation process and multi-asset strategy products belong solely to the realm of quants. We do not agree. We believe that the multi-asset investing process can benefit all investment professionals. In turn, the profession can deliver better results for investors. For example, top-down asset allocators can obviously benefit from an enhanced process of asset allocation. Managers of single-asset portfolios can also learn how their "slice" fits into the big picture.

Another important source of efficiency gain may come from breaking down the barriers between quants, who are often in top-down roles, and fundamental investors, who tend to run bottom-up portfolios. The current practice of quants making asset allocation decisions on the basis of their understanding (or lack thereof) of the underlying funds is inherently inefficient. The process that Dennis Stattman and his team have developed can be quite revealing in this regard.

To make this book accessible to all investment professionals, we have asked our contributors, including some of the top quants, to explain the concepts in plain English with no formulas. We have also attempted to demystify multi-asset investing by providing case studies, in which some of the best-known portfolio managers explain how they have successfully run multi-asset portfolios. Despite the fact that they all have their own unique approaches—some more quantitative and others more fundamental—they all follow at least some of the same philosophy that we share in this book.

The popularity of multi-asset strategies has grown steadily in recent years because they serve important functions by satisfying long-term investors' demand for investment solutions. As a provider of investment management education, we are particularly pleased that CFA® charterholders learn about multi-asset investing in the CFA Program. As professionals, however, we must stay current with the latest developments.

I thank our contributors for collaborating with us on this important initiative. Larry Cao, CFA, and his colleagues have done an admirable job of putting this project together and seeing it through to completion. We look forward to the day when the entire profession embraces multi-asset investing so that we can do an even better job of serving investors' needs. We will be more than satisfied if this book helps you in any way on your professional journey.

Paul Smith, CFA, President and CEO, CFA Institute

CONTENTS

PART II
CASE STUDIES AND MANAGER INTERVIEWS

ABOUT THE AUTHORS

Gregory C. Allen is the chief executive officer, chief risk officer, and president of Callan, one of the largest independently owned investment consulting firms in the United States. He oversees the firm's fund sponsor consulting, trust advisory, and all research and education groups that include global manager research, alternative investment research, capital markets research, database, client report services, operations, and the Callan Institute. Greg is a member of Callan's Management Committee, Alternatives Review Committee, Institute Advisory Committee, and Client Policy Review Committee, as well as the Investment Committee, which oversees all of Callan's discretionary multi-manager solutions. He is also a member of Callan's board of directors and is a shareholder of the firm. Greg joined Callan's San Francisco office in 1988 as an analyst where he focused on capital market research, asset allocation and liability analysis, and manager structure analysis. In 1993, he took over Callan's Operations and Capital Markets Research groups where he oversaw the complete redesign and implementation of Callan's database management and performance measurement systems. In 2000, Greg was promoted to director of research, and in 2007 was promoted to president. He took on the CEO role in 2017.

Larry Cao, CFA, conducts original research and develops educational products with a focus on the investment industry in his capacity as director of content for Asia Pacific at CFA Institute. Larry has 20 years of experience in the investment industry. Before joining CFA Institute, Larry worked at HSBC as senior manager for the Asia Pacific region. He started his career at the People's Bank of China as a USD fixed-income portfolio manager. He also worked for US asset managers Munder Capital Management, managing US and international equity portfolios (winning a Lipper Award in the process), and Morningstar/Ibbotson Associates, managing multi-asset investment programs for a global financial institution clientele. Larry has been interviewed by a wide range of global and regional media outlets, including Bloomberg, CNN, the *Financial Times, South China Morning Post*, and *Wall Street*

Journal. He is also a frequent speaker at conferences on such topics as fintech and multi-asset investing. He has led the development of a number of CFA Institute publications on these subjects, including the CFA Institute report *FinTech 2017: China, Asia, and Beyond*. Larry received his MBA from the University of Notre Dame. He was also a visiting scholar at the MIT Sloan School of Management.

Jason Hsu is founder and CIO of Rayliant Global Advisors, a quantitative and fundamental asset manager specializing in Chinese equities. Jason also co-founded Research Affiliates, which is a 160B asset manager specializing in smart beta indexes and asset allocation. Jason sits on the editorial boards of the *Financial Analysts Journal, Journal of Investment Management, Journal of Investment Consulting*, and *Journal of Index Investing*. Jason is an adjunct professor of finance at UCLA Anderson Business School and holds a visiting professorship at both Kyoto University in Japan and National Chengchi University in Taiwan. Jason is the author of over 40 journal articles and is a contributing author of eight handbooks on finance and economics. Jason's research has won two Graham and Dodd Scroll Awards from CFA Institute, two Bernstein Fabozzi/Jacobs Levy Outstanding Research Awards, and three William Sharpe Best Research Awards. Jason was recognized by Institutional Investor in 2008 as one of the 20 rising stars of the industry. His co-invention of the Fundamental Index won an award for best index from *Global Pensions* magazine in 2007, 2008, and 2009. Jason received his PhD in finance from UCLA Anderson Business School, his MS from Stanford, and his BS from Caltech.

Tham Chiew Kit is head of total portfolio strategy (TPS) in the Economics & Investment Strategy (EIS) department at GIC Singapore. He leads TPS in providing recommendations to GIC management, the board, and the client regarding the construction and management of the GIC portfolio and its active strategies. In particular, TPS provides market assessment and portfolio analysis to support GIC management and the GIC board in their investment decisions. The team helps management evaluate the GIC active portfolio and its specific strategies in light of market opportunities and risks. The team continues to work closely with the client to define its investment objectives and risk tolerance and to formulate strategic asset allocation for the board's approval. Chiew Kit and his team play a pivotal role in the conceptualization and implementation of the "new investment framework." Chiew Kit joined GIC in 1993 as a senior economist in the Economics department. In 1994, he was transferred to the Foreign Exchange department, where he spent six years, with his last-held position there as a senior investment manager. In 2001, after a stint at Morgan Stanley, Chiew Kit returned to GIC's Foreign Exchange department and was subsequently deployed to the Investment Policy & Strategy (IPS) department in 2004. In 2011, Chiew Kit was appointed head of strategic asset allocation (SAA) in the newly formed EIS, following the merger of the IPS and Economics & Strategy departments. As head of SAA, he advised management and the client on asset allocation and investment strategy. Chiew Kit earned a BA in economics (with second upper-class honors) in 1985 and an MA in economics in 1989 from Cambridge University. The Singapore Public Service Commission awarded him its President's Scholarship in 1982.

Darius Liu, CFA, is vice president of total portfolio strategy (TPS) in the Economics & Investment Strategy (EIS) department at GIC Singapore. TPS provides recommendations to GIC's management, board, and clients on issues related to asset allocation and portfolio construction. In particular, TPS aims to construct and recommend the optimal total portfolio that meets GIC's investment objective by allocating GIC's capital across a variety of asset classes and active strategies. TPS reviews GIC's policy and active portfolios regularly to ensure they remain optimal in light of changing market conditions and risks. Within TPS, Darius focuses on the analysis and evaluation of public equity, private equity, infrastructure, and factor-based investment strategies. Darius joined GIC in January 2013 as a vice president in the Human Resource and Organization department, where he was responsible for conceptualizing various HR and organizational development initiatives across the GIC group. Darius transferred to the TPS team in the EIS department in January 2015. Before joining GIC, Darius was the head of strategic and operational planning at the Singapore Ministry of Defence, where he spearheaded the establishment of the organization's strategic planning and capability development framework. Darius was also responsible for developing the oversight mechanism for the organization's budget and resource allocation mechanisms. Before his stint at the Ministry of Defence, Darius served in the Singapore Ministry of Finance, where he supported the review of GIC's investment policy and worked on various issues related to the management of Singapore's financial reserves. Darius was awarded a Singapore Public Service Commission Overseas Merit Scholarship in 2000. He graduated summa cum laude from Cornell University with a BS in mechanical engineering in 2003 and obtained an MS in mechanical engineering from Cornell in 2004. He also holds an MS in financial engineering from the National University of Singapore. Darius is a CFA charterholder and a CAIA charterholder.

Jeffrey Ptak, CFA, is head of global manager research at Morningstar Research Services LLC, a wholly owned subsidiary of Morningstar, Inc. Before assuming his current role in 2015, Jeffrey was president and chief investment officer of Morningstar Investment Services, Inc.—an investment unit that provides managed portfolio services through fee-based, independent financial advisers—for six years. Jeffrey joined Morningstar in 2002 as a senior mutual fund analyst and has also served as an equity analyst, director of ETF analysis, and editor of *Morningstar ETFInvestor*. He briefly left Morningstar to become an investment products analyst for William Blair & Company, and earlier in his career, he was a manager at Arthur Andersen. Jeffrey holds a bachelor's degree in accounting from the University of Wisconsin and is a CFA charterholder.

Brian Singer, CFA, is head of the Dynamic Allocation Strategies (DAS) team at William Blair & Company, where he also serves as a portfolio manager. In this role, Brian shares with Thomas Clarke ultimate responsibility for strategy setting and portfolio construction across all DAS portfolios. Before joining William Blair in 2011, Brian was the head of investment strategies at Singer Partners, LLC. Before that, he was head of global investment solutions and chief investment officer for the Americas at UBS Global Asset Management, where he was a member of the UBS Group's managing board and the Global Asset Management Executive Committee. Brian is extensively involved with CFA Institute. He is a member of both the CFA Society Chicago and the CFA Institute Research Foundation Board of Regents. In 2015, he received the CFA Institute Distinguished Service Award, which recognizes CFA members who have made a significant contribution to CFA Institute through their leadership, exceptional stewardship, and outstanding service. He formerly served as a board member and chair of the CFA Institute Board of Governors. Brian has written extensively on global portfolio, currency, and performance issues and co-wrote the seminal *Determinants of Portfolio Performance II: An Update* with Gary Brinson and Gilbert Beebower. In 2009, he was the lead author of *Investment Leadership and Portfolio Management* (Wiley Publishing). In 2015, Brian was inducted into the Performance and Risk Management Hall of Fame by the Spaulding Group. He serves on the Endowment Investment Committee at Exeter College of Oxford University. Brian is chair of the "Free to Choose Network," which is inspired by the ideas of economist Milton Friedman, and he is a board member of the Rehabilitation Institute of Chicago Foundation. He has a BA in economics from Northwestern University and an MBA from the University of Chicago's Booth School of Business.

Leslie Teo, CFA, is director of the Economics & Investment Strategy (EIS) department and chief economist at GIC Singapore. He oversees the economics and investment strategy team at GIC. The team is responsible for asset allocation, total portfolio construction, and identification of key long-term trends that would affect GIC's portfolio. Leslie holds a BA from the University of Chicago and a PhD in economics from the University of Rochester. He is a certified financial risk manager and is also a CFA charterholder. Prior to joining GIC, Leslie was at the International Monetary Fund, where he worked in the Asia Pacific, Monetary and Financial Systems, Policy Development and Review, and European II departments. Leslie was also head of the Financial Surveillance Division at the Monetary Authority of Singapore.

Phillip Wool is vice president of equity research at Rayliant Global Advisors, a quantitative and fundamental asset manager specializing in Chinese equities. Before joining Rayliant, Phillip was an assistant professor of finance at SUNY Buffalo, where he conducted research on quantitative trading strategies and investor behavior and taught investment management. Prior to entering academia, Phillip worked as a research analyst covering alternative investments at Hammond Associates, an institutional fund consultant. Phillip received his PhD in finance from the UCLA Anderson School of Management. He received an AB in economics and a BSBA in finance and accounting from Washington University in St. Louis.

INTRODUCTION

Despite the popularity of multi-asset strategies, especially after the global financial crisis in 2008, very few books have been written about the topic. The few books available, with their heavy use of mathematical formulas, are intended mostly for quants. There appears to be a void in terms of a multi-asset investing book for the majority of investors. This book is our attempt to fill that void.

When we first discussed this project with Paul Smith, CFA, president and CEO of CFA Institute, Paul's advice was that we should aim to produce *the* book on the subject, not just *a* book. This is our first attempt at achieving that goal.

We focused on three features in putting this book together: (1) concise: each chapter is short enough to be read in 15–20 minutes, (2) accessible: the book is written in plain English and is entirely formula-free, and (3) authoritative: we have engaged the help of some of the brightest minds in this area from around the world. If our readers think we have succeeded in these three endeavors, we shall be quite content.

HOW IS THIS BOOK ORGANIZED?

This book is about both concepts and practices in multi-asset investing. Part I focuses on two important concepts. Part II includes a few institutional case studies.

Chapter 1 sets the stage for the entire book. It explains the types of products under the multi-asset umbrella, highlighting how (properly managed) multi-asset-strategy products are different from the more traditional balanced funds and funds of funds.

In Chapter 2, Jason Hsu and Phillip Wool discuss how risk factor allocation can add value for investors who use asset classes in their asset allocation analysis. Although quants may find talking about this concept challenging without formulas, the two authors do just that.

For the more quantitatively inclined, references to the more advanced papers are included.

In Chapter 3, Brian Singer, CFA, examines the role of both dynamic asset allocation (DAA) and tactical asset allocation using his overall investment taxonomy. DAA is a challenging topic, and a significant number of investors confuse it with market timing. Brian disputes that misperception, citing authorities ranging from John Maynard Keynes to Gary Brinson.

We dedicate Chapter 4 to risk parity, given its popularity among investors. Greg Allen analyzes both the theory and the historical performance of risk parity and provides a balanced and convincing assessment of the strategy.

Risk factor allocation has long been the domain of academics and quants. The Morningstar Style Box is an intuitive illustration of how average investors can put the concept to use in their daily investing. In Chapter 5, Jeff Ptak looks under the hood and gives readers an overview of both the methodology and the application of this useful tool for retail investors.

The last three chapters focus on real-life investor stories: A prominent Asian sovereign wealth manager and two veteran portfolio managers share their experiences in managing multi-asset portfolios.

A key theme that we try to convey is that all roads lead to Rome. There is no single "best" or even "right" way to manage multi-asset strategies. And getting started does not require that you possess all the needed skills (of course, the more edge you have, the more likely you are to succeed).

In Chapter 6, three GIC senior executives present GIC's well-structured approach. GIC's focus on the long term is an important feature and is appropriate given the long-term nature of its portfolio. GIC's risk-and-return targets clearly reflect its emphasis on growing purchasing power over the long run.

Chapter 7 consists of an interview with Dennis Stattman, CFA, a veteran portfolio manager at BlackRock. Dennis started managing global asset allocation funds as early as 1989 and is a true pioneer in the field. He goes into the details of how he manages the products as well as how he has performed over the years. We believe the conversation to be deeply rewarding and hope our readers agree.

The book's final chapter comprises a conversation with Ben Inker, CFA, a longtime portfolio manager at GMO who took over asset allocation products from Jeremy Grantham, the famed founder of the firm. Ben has a rather unique approach to investing, in general, and multi-asset strategies, in particular, that is rooted in both economic analysis and fundamental analysis and is implemented with a quantitative flair.

WHO SHOULD READ THIS BOOK?

This book is written with investment decision makers in mind. Our aim is to provide a guide for those decision makers who are not already intimately familiar with the concepts and practices of multi-asset investing. Even today, asset allocation seems to be mainly the domain of quants. But a large majority of investors are not quants, and many have not embraced multi-asset investing for that reason. So, we made a conscious decision to tell our story entirely free of formulas.

Another decision we made was to keep each chapter short so it can be read in 15–20 minutes. And the chapters can largely be read independently, not necessarily in the order presented. Our reason is obvious: Investors are busy people. We think that this approach is the only way the book will be consumed by our target audience.

We thank each author for his effort. (As the saying goes, I have made this longer than usual because I have not had time to make it shorter. Authors know this all too well.)

In sum, this book is intended for investors who have not taken full advantage of multi-asset investing (we think all investors should), either because of a lack of quantitative training or because they are too busy to stay current on the latest trends.

Readers who fit any of the following profiles should find this book helpful:

- Chief investment officers who want to update their knowledge of current developments in multi-asset investing
- Portfolio managers and analysts who work with a product that is only one part of a multi-asset portfolio and wish to better understand how it fits into the big picture
- Salespersons, product managers, and client portfolio managers who want to learn the latest trends in multi-asset investing so they can better communicate with their target audiences
- Wealth managers who wish to benefit from the latest institutional approaches to multi-asset investing
- Retail investors who want to take advantage of industry knowledge and manage their own investments
- Regulators who would like to stay abreast of industry developments
- Professors who teach—and the students who take—advanced investment courses
- Corporate and college libraries wishing to acquire an investment book that all investors can use

In terms of level of difficulty, Chapter 1 is intended for investors of all levels. The remainder of the book should prove interesting to both midlevel investment professionals and advanced investors.

I'd like to thank my CFA Institute colleagues Paul Smith, Nitin Mehta, Nick Pollard, Rob Gowen, Joey Chan, Julie Hammond, Glenn Doggett, Tom Berry, Joyce Chan, Missy Tierney, and intern Natalie Wong for their support of and assistance with this project. I thank my co-authors for their contributions. I'd also like to thank the panelists at a few panels that I chaired at industry events in 2014, and Myron Scholes, chief strategist at Janus Henderson, who met with us in 2015. Discussions I had with Dr. Scholes and the panelists, including Richard Brandweiner, CFA, CIO of First State Super at the time and a partner at Leapfrog

Investments now; Thomas Franzen, chief strategist at AP2, a Swedish pension fund; Dong Ik Lee, former CIO at KIC and Director General at AIIB now; and Nachcha Protpakorn, Deputy Secretary General at the Thai Government Pension Fund, played an important role in shaping our thoughts that formed the basis of my writings included in our earlier publication, "Managing Multi-Asset Strategies."

For experienced multi-asset researchers and practitioners who would like to contribute to our multi-asset efforts by writing or speaking in the future, please feel free to get in touch with us by emailing larry.cao@cfainstitute.org.

PART I

NEW FRONTIERS IN ASSET ALLOCATION AND PORTFOLIO CONSTRUCTION

1. ESSENTIALS OF MULTI-ASSET INVESTING

Larry Cao, CFA

Multi-asset strategy is the latest name that the investment management industry has adopted for what has long been known as a balanced fund. Although products under the new name are not automatically managed under a new process—much less with any guarantee of higher returns or better risk diversification—I use the term to refer to what I believe to be a new paradigm of investment management: namely, the holistic view that investment decision makers take in looking after investors' portfolios.

In the sections below, I explain (1) the various types of products for multi-asset strategies, (2) the key players in the multi-asset investing process and their respective roles, and (3) key differentiators in managing a multi-asset strategy that sets it apart from an average balanced fund.

1.1. TYPES OF MULTI-ASSET STRATEGIES

Multi-asset strategy refers to the type of investment strategy that involves investing in various asset classes. Typically, a multi-asset strategy uses an asset allocation program on top of the substrategies that invest in individual asset classes.

I have intentionally made this definition very flexible to encompass all the possible scenarios that are highlighted below.

The old *balanced funds* were typically put together by combining a (core) stock fund and a (core) bond fund with some cash as a cushion. Over time, core stock and bond funds evolved into funds of multiple (sub)asset classes. The main difference of this "new" breed of funds from the balanced funds is reflected most in the increased number of (sub)asset classes. In many cases, these funds simply kept the old balanced fund moniker, although *fund of funds (FOF)* has become a popular name over the last 10 or 15 years.

More recently, especially since the global financial crisis, these products have been increasingly sold under the *multi-asset strategy* name. Many have adopted a dynamic asset allocation process, which was less common prior to the global financial crisis.

The four “main” asset classes covered by multi-asset strategies are stocks, bonds, alternatives, and cash. Within each, there are multiple ways to slice and dice them.

Stock funds can be managed according to size (large-, mid-, small-, and micro-cap), style (growth and value), sector (consumer, financials, health care, industrials, technology, etc.), and geography (Asia, Europe, Latin America, Japan, BRIC, etc.).

Bond funds can be managed according to duration (long, intermediate, and short term), credit (core, government, credit, high yield, etc.), geography (global, United States, emerging markets, etc.), and currency (US dollar, euro, and local currency).

Alternatives include various hedge strategies, infrastructure, private equity, and real estate, many of which are common in *institutional* multi-asset strategies. *Retail* programs generally cannot include many types of alternatives owing to liquidity and regulatory constraints.

This broad definition of multi-asset-strategy fund also covers strategies that intentionally cover only a limited segment of the entire universe. This “limited” segment can be anything—for example, alternatives or international equities. They were developed largely to fill the capability gap of some asset owners and fund houses in certain segments of the market.

The fund of hedge funds (FoHF) would certainly qualify as such. The rationale for having such a fund is simple: With the sole objective of creating alpha, hedge funds can have attractive performance, but at times, they can also be volatile. FoHF is the hedge fund industry’s attempt to address mainstream investors’ need for better returns with less volatility.

Funds of hedge funds are also called multi-strategy hedge funds. This is where it may get slightly confusing. Multi-strategy funds can be a special case of the broadly defined multi-asset strategy; the bulk of multi-asset strategies would involve multiple asset classes but not necessarily hedge funds.

The *target-date fund*, popular in the United States, is also a type of multi-asset strategy. The difference from a typical multi-asset-strategy fund is that target-date funds have an asset allocation that varies with the time, or "target date," of withdrawal. To differentiate, the industry has coined the term *target-risk fund* to refer to the "old school" fund of funds.

1.2. MANAGERS OF AND INVESTORS IN MULTI-ASSET STRATEGIES

Multi-asset strategy came into existence for two reasons. First, partly driven by demand for product differentiation, the number of asset classes has exploded over recent decades since the initial proliferation of the product category. Second, tactical asset allocation came into fashion after the global financial crisis, and the name—multi-asset strategy—partly implies (accurately or inaccurately) more flexibility with the asset allocation component of these strategies.

Demand for the product comes from all types of investors, although institutional investors tend to be more powerful in influencing the product's development and future direction.

One could argue that every investor, institutional or retail, has its own multi-asset product, which is the entire investment portfolio. Institutional investors are, on average, better at grasping this concept.

The largest investors in these products are asset owners, such as sovereign wealth funds, pension funds, insurance companies, and endowment funds. Adoption among private wealth managers and retail investors, especially in more-developed markets, is also substantial.

The supply for the products comes from various sources. Asset managers are clearly the dominant force. Many asset owners hire consulting firms to manage the multi-asset-strategy products for them. The consultants generally develop asset allocation programs and then select appropriate asset managers to implement them. They manage significant sums of money for their clients, although their mandate often limits their level of discretion in the investment process.

Before looking at all the players' roles and the necessary skills to perform, let's first delve into a decision faced by the asset owners that blurs the line between manager and investor. That decision is whether to outsource.

Multi-asset strategies are the decathlons of the investment industry. They require practically all the investment skills one can think of, from securities selection at the individual asset class level to the overall asset allocation. Among all the multi-asset-strategy products on the market today, the vast majority are managed by multiple teams because one rarely finds all the required skills in one place—especially in today's world, where investment talent has become highly specialized.

The outsourcing decision depends on access to the required skills in an investment organization. Unless you have proven skills in a particular stage of multi-asset investing, hiring external managers for that particular role seems the natural solution. And unless you have tremendous skills in trading operations and/or running extremely large sums of money, you should probably also not be doing your own index investing because the top vendors in the business would have a tremendous cost advantage.

External managers are used more often in such areas as alternatives that tend to require very special knowledge of particular investments. When a domestically focused fund expands overseas, it is also common to engage external managers or adopt index solutions. Managers, of course, will adapt to the specific challenges they face.

The Korean Investment Corporation outsources about a third of its publicly traded securities and all of its alternatives.[1] AP2, one of Sweden's pension funds, has a slightly different twist. "When expanding outside of Sweden, we hired external managers, which turned out less successful than we hoped. We have since developed tilted indices and took assets in-house using a quantitative process. The exception is alternatives—all [are] managed externally," said AP2's Tomas Franzén.[2]

Scott Anderson, CFA, head of equity research for Japan at Russell Investments, discussed the firm's manager search process. "We try to understand qualitatively . . . their approach on top of conducting quantitative analysis of performance data and see if they are consistent. In particular, we screen for poor performance and see whether that can be explained by the philosophy." Anderson believes that it is important to distinguish between luck and skill. "Being contrarian and delivering solid performance is a good indication of skill," Anderson added.[3]

In addition to skills, resource availability is another variable that comes into play in the outsourcing decision. Large asset owners with abundant resources are most likely to build in-house capabilities, whereas the less fortunate ones may resort to outsourcing for cost reasons.

Most asset owners tend to adopt a mixed model in managing their investments—that is, they manage some assets and functions in-house and outsource the others to external managers. So, in most cases, they are both investors and managers.

Sovereign wealth funds (SWFs) have been an important force in shaping multi-asset strategies. They are state-owned investment funds with a broad, often global investment mandate. Incidentally, SWFs started to gain public attention around the same time as multi-asset strategies. Given their substantial resources, they both have a strong need for global diversification and access to talents required

[1] Larry Cao, "Managing Multi-Asset Strategies," *Enterprising Investor* (CFA Institute blog), vol. 2016, no. 1 (May 2016): 5 (https://www.cfainstitute.org/learning/products/publications/eic/Pages/eic.v1.n1.aspx/).
[2] Cao, "Managing Multi-Asset Strategies," 5.
[3] Cao, "Managing Multi-Asset Strategies," 5.

to properly manage a large portion of these products. They tend to do their asset allocation in-house and use external managers only in asset classes requiring unique skills that are tough to get in their local markets.

Endowments are best known among asset owners who embraced multi-asset investing long before the term was coined. Endowments involve financial assets, typically donated to such not-for-profit institutions as universities. The institutions can generally use the returns from the investments but not the principal. This feature has made the duration of endowments the longest among asset owners, and multi-asset strategies are a natural fit for their investment needs.

Their long-term nature allows them the flexibility to invest in alternative assets, such as private equity and direct real estate. This is an important distinguishing feature of the so-called Yale model.[4] But the need for international diversification is not nearly as strong for SWFs, given that the bulk of a university's expenses are domestic.

Pension funds have gone through many changes in recent decades. The switch to the defined contribution regime from defined benefits has particular implications for our discussion here. For defined contribution plans, pension funds play the role of an administrator, but often they are also charged with selecting the funds to be made available on the platform. Multi-asset funds with embedded asset allocations are among the alternatives.

The industry has long embraced the 60/40 model for pension asset allocation (i.e., 60% equity and 40% fixed income). This rule of thumb remains popular in the defined contribution world.

Insurance companies are important investors in multi-asset strategies. Liabilities of life insurers have very long durations, allowing them to invest in long-duration assets. Regulations, however, require that they have enough assets in fixed income to maintain liquidity in the face of

[4]David F. Swensen, *Pioneering Portfolio Management: An Unconventional Approach to Institutional Investment* (New York: Free Press, 2009).

adverse events. Property insurers face much more uncertainty. So, as a whole, high allocation to fixed-income instruments is an important attribute of the insurers' portfolios.

An exception is variable annuity (VA) policies. VA policies are like the defined contribution plans in the pension world, where individual policyholders can choose among various alternatives in asset allocation and funds to invest in while leaving the task of selecting managers to the insurer.

Pension funds and insurance companies are far more likely to hire consultants and external managers than SWFs and endowments. Despite Warren Buffett's stellar performance at Berkshire Hathaway, insurance companies' core competence is generally not in managing investments. Consultants develop asset allocation programs for their pension and insurance clients as well as select funds that can be used to implement these programs. In this manner, the top-tier consulting firms often have influence over who gets access to pension plan and insurance assets worth hundreds of billions of dollars. It tends to be an indirect influence though, because ultimately the choice of funds and the timing of getting in and out of those funds are not entirely at their discretion.

In contrast, mutual funds are truly managers of multi-asset portfolios in the sense that investors give fund managers discretion over their funds. Mutual funds use different models to manage multi-asset portfolios, dating back to the early days of the balanced funds. Typically, the underlying funds are in-house funds that focus on a slice of the entire market; there is a separate top-down process—ranging from sophisticated quantitative methods to a rule of thumb that relies more on the team's experience—for allocating assets to the individual funds. These functions are generally performed by different teams within the fund house, although we know of at least one case where the entire process is carried out by a single team.[5]

[5]See Chapter 7.

Mutual funds and funds carried by pension plans and insurance companies need to be marked to market daily, which rules out their participation in many such alternative asset classes as private equity and venture capital funds, where investments generally need to be committed for five to seven years.

Private wealth managers' level of sophistication in multi-asset investing varies widely, depending on the market they operate in, the asset level, and their product access. At one end of the spectrum are large family offices in developed markets and private bankers at top-tier financial institutions, who can be as competent as some of their institutional investor peers. At the other end are many investors, largely retail and often in emerging and frontier markets, who have yet to take a holistic view in managing their entire investment portfolios. If the risk-and-return profiles of their investment portfolios turn out to be close to optimal, that is pure serendipity.

1.3. PERFORMANCE EVALUATION IN THE MULTI-ASSET CONTEXT

Before addressing what differentiates multi-asset strategies, I will discuss the evaluation of multi-asset strategies in general. After all, without a consensus on what makes a "good" multi-asset strategy, we cannot have a meaningful comparison of different strategies.

Proper performance measurement, attribution, and appraisal can enhance the probability of success for the entire investment process. Improper evaluation can directly create some of the oft-criticized issues in the investment industry. For example, Nobel laureate Myron Scholes believes that benchmark and tracking error can derail an investment process.[6]

A particularly tricky point in comparing multi-asset strategies is how to group funds with different allocations to equity. When markets are performing well, the allocation to equity tends to dominate stock selection in terms of impact on total portfolio return.

[6]Cao, "Managing Multi-Asset Strategies," 13.

Despite the implementation challenges, modern portfolio theory (MPT) seems the most relevant framework for investors in multi-asset strategies. The risk and return objectives of the GIC and Thai government pension funds (GPFs) are good examples. The "best" funds are the efficient portfolios, and the next-best funds are on the next parallel curve below, and so on.

Unfortunately, investors and thus the industry are far more focused on return than risk; as a result, we end up with a system that compares fund performances within a range of equity allocations. The range tends to be too wide and may encourage managers to bet on a higher equity allocation if they believe equities will outperform in the long run and, maybe, more frequently in the short run. This is one of the reasons why multi-asset funds' performance rankings are far more controversial than pure equity or bond funds.

Multi-asset strategies are intended to serve investors' long-term goals. Many underlying investment managers also follow investment processes that are inherently long term. For example, value strategies often take a full market cycle to bear fruit. If investors hold such managers to a quarterly evaluation cycle, conflicts often arise. Understandably, such managers' returns may end up in the bottom quartile in a given quarter. Investors expecting otherwise will be disappointed. Worse, if the managers are forced to modify their process and deliver more consistent returns, they might become disoriented.

Smart investors have come up with different approaches to deal with this potential conflict. In short, measuring a multi-asset strategy's long-term performance over inflation and short-term volatility relative to a simple equity plus fixed-income reference portfolio seems to help motivate managers to resolve the conflict between long-term goals and short-term evaluation cycles.

According to Tham Chiew Kit, a managing director at GIC, the sovereign wealth fund measures its own performance over a 20-year horizon.[7] He thinks the 65% equity/35% bond reference portfolio is more

[7]Cao, "Managing Multi-Asset Strategies," 10.

appropriate as a risk measure than as a short-term return yardstick. He admits that external active managers have a much tighter leash, although private market managers are allowed more time to demonstrate their competence.

The success of the Thai GPF is judged by its performance relative to the consumer price index (CPI) over 10 years, says Nachcha Protpakorn, deputy secretary general of the Thai GPF.[8] They also measure the portfolio's performance against a global benchmark that is reset each year opportunistically.

1.4. DIFFERENTIATING FACTORS

I now discuss what separates the current breed of multi-asset strategies from the not-so-old funds of funds and the older balance funds.

I believe that the leading multi-asset products have been enhanced in at least one of two ways compared with other multi-asset managers, especially strategies for funds of funds and balanced funds: risk factor allocation and dynamic asset allocation. All else being equal, having a competence in either or both areas gives investment teams an edge over those who do not.

Risk factor allocation can trace its roots to developments that started as early as the 1970s, from both an academic and a practitioner perspective. Stephen Ross's arbitrage pricing theory (APT),[9] a major post-CAPM theoretical development, became the conceptual framework for understanding and applying risk factor analysis.[10] Another milestone

---

[8]Cao, "Managing Multi-Asset Strategies," 10.

[9]Stephen Ross, "The Arbitrage Theory of Capital Asset Pricing," *Journal of Economic Theory*, vol. 13, no. 3 (December 1976): 341–360.

[10]Stephen Ross et al., *A Practitioner's Guide to Factor Models* (Charlottesville, VA: Research Foundation of the Institute of Chartered Financial Analysts, 1994): http://www.cfapubs.org/doi/abs/10.2470/rf.v1994.n4.4445.

development was the Fama–French three-factor model[11] that eventually won Eugene Fama the Nobel Prize.

The earliest experiments in applying factor analysis to investment management were also carried out, or at least assisted by, academics. Pioneers in this field include such (in)famous quants as Barr Rosenberg, who later founded BARRA.[12] The firm not only consulted for institutional investors but also developed a suite of off-the-shelf analytical tools by the name of BARRA (now part of MSCI) that has become nearly synonymous with the idea of risk factor analysis. The outgrowth of constant research and updates, the latest off-the-shelf risk factor models incorporate an extensive suite of risk factors that covers not only US equities but also fixed income and practically all major financial markets.

As implied by APT, there is no single perfect risk factor model. In addition to the three-factor model and the more extensive Barra-type models, there are other ways to measure portfolio risk. For example, Northfield developed a model whose factors are all macroeconomic variables, which provides a different perspective for evaluating portfolio risk.

The term *factor investing* has become rather popular in the industry in recent years. Although it loosely covers the same or similar topics as *risk factor allocation*, I prefer the latter term because I believe the industry has rightly shifted its focus from the return aspect of risk premiums in the early days to the risk aspect today. For example, one of the multi-asset managers' favorite topics remains "avoiding unintended bets." This is one of the most important ways that risk factor analysis is being integrated into the investment process.

Compared with risk factor analysis, dynamic asset allocation is more controversial among both practitioners and researchers. Although

---

[11]Eugene F. Fama and Kenneth R. French, "Common Risk Factors in the Returns on Stocks and Bonds," *Journal of Financial Economics*, vol. 33, no. 1 (February 1993): 3–56.
[12]Barry B. Burr, "Barr Rosenberg," *Pensions & Investments* (27 October 2003): http://www.pionline.com/article/20031027/PRINT/310270759/barr-rosenberg.

most marketers are more than happy to explain to you how their products incorporate a dynamic element into their investment process, many portfolio managers are just as happy to tell you that they do not rely on it.

A white paper produced by a fund house summarizing the popular methodologies for dynamic asset allocation could provide some clues as to the reason why.[13] Asset allocation is a more challenging task than security selection for quants partly because there are only a small number of factors at work, so the risk of getting it wrong at any one time is higher.

Despite the practical challenges, the potential benefits of dynamic asset allocation are substantial. "We have got a model for cross-section diversification. We have to balance that with time-series diversification because, when time diversification fails, cross-section diversification fails too," said Myron Scholes at an event in Tokyo sponsored by CFA Society Japan.[14] "The greatest reward comes from time diversification," Scholes observed. I agree. For example, the best move most investors could have made in this lifetime is probably switching out of equities into US Treasuries in 2008.

Multi-asset investing is a strategy in which practically all types of investment skills can be put to use, be they fundamental or quantitative, stocks or bonds, Asia or the United States. There are no hard and fast rules when it comes to what works in managing multi-asset strategies. Although that sounds demanding, it also means that a multi-asset product with an edge in any aspect can potentially do better than the average, which, in this context, means the market portfolio. A myth about multi-asset investing is that it is supposed to be passive. That is true only for investment teams that believe they have no edge in investing. Where you do have an edge, you should make that element active. Three main aspects can be made active. The first is strategic

---

[13]Yesim Tokat and Kimberly A. Stockton, "A Primer on Tactical Asset Allocation Strategy Evaluation," *Vanguard Investment Counseling & Research* (2010): https://personal.vanguard.com/pdf/flgtaa.pdf.
[14]Cao, "Managing Multi-Asset Strategies," 13.

asset allocation, or a reference portfolio.[15] The second is dynamic asset allocation, or rotation strategies. And last but not least is security selection.

The omnipotent investor possessing all the skills required for managing multi-asset products probably does not exist (although CFA charterholders, who must pass stringent tests in all the main investment disciplines, seem uniquely well prepared for the task). I know of only one team that does not outsource any part of the investment decision making.[16] So, there is no doubt that this is a challenging task. At the same time, I think that is also what makes multi-asset investing so fascinating. There is much room for improvement, for the entire profession to contribute. Ultimately, there is nothing more rewarding than serving our clients well, and it is clearer than ever that what clients need is the full package. They need results. A multi-asset strategy is the ideal solution for incorporating all the skills that we possess to deliver just that.

REFERENCES

Cao, Larry. 2016. "Managing Multi-Asset Strategies." Charlottesville, VA: CFA Institute: https://www.cfainstitute.org/learning/products/publications/eic/Pages/eic.v1.n1.aspx.

CFA Institute Research Foundation. 1994. *A Practitioner's Guide to Factor Models*. Charlottesville, VA: CFA Institute Research Foundation: http://www.cfapubs.org/doi/abs/10.2470/rf.v1994.n4.4445.

Fama, Eugene F., and Kenneth R. French. 1993. "Common Risk Factors in the Returns on Stocks and Bonds." *Journal of Financial Economics*, vol. 33, no.1 (February): 3–56.

Ross, Stephen. 1976. "The Arbitrage Theory of Capital Asset Pricing." *Journal of Economic Theory*, vol. 13, no. 3: 341–360.

[15]For a detailed discussion of reference portfolios, see Chapter 6.
[16]For more details on the BlackRock Global Asset Allocation Fund, see Chapter 7.

Swensen, David F. 2009. *Pioneering Portfolio Management: An Unconventional Approach to Institutional Investment.* New York: Free Press.

Tokat, Yesim, and Kimberly A. Stockton. 2010. "A Primer on Tactical Asset Allocation Strategy Evaluation." Vanguard: https://personal.vanguard.com/pdf/flgtaa.pdf.

2. RISK FACTOR ALLOCATION

Jason Hsu
Phillip Wool

2.1. FACTOR VS. ASSET ALLOCATION

The traditional asset allocation framework, unsurprisingly, starts with assets. This tradition is based on convenience and, perhaps, an implicit assumption that key asset classes match well with important risk exposures. The modern asset allocation and analytic framework anchors on "factors."[1] Although the two frameworks may lead to similar outcomes, the factor-based approach offers greater simplicity—once investors master the factor-related nomenclature—and allows for a more natural asset allocation intuition. In this chapter, we explain the benefits of the factor-based approach relative to the asset-based approach and introduce a set of simplifying analogies that facilitates building intuition about the differences between the two approaches. Toward the end of the chapter, we provide four applications of the factor-based framework to demonstrate investment issues that are not apparent under an asset-based analytical framework. We conclude with some cautionary comments that explore more nuanced issues associated with factor-based portfolio allocation. A complete description of how to implement a factor-based approach, however, is outside the scope of this chapter.

2.2. ASSET CLASSES VS. FACTOR EXPOSURES

In the asset-based framework, the allocation process entails assigning weights to various asset classes available to the investor (e.g., equities, bonds, commodities, real estate). Asset classes are captured by their corresponding market indexes. For example, MSCI ACWI (All Country World Index) and FTSE All World Index are often used to represent the global equity asset class. Each major asset category is

[1]The modern approach has grown out of the literature on arbitrage pricing theory (Ross 1976) and subsequent refinements of the model's risk factors into meaningful economic risk exposures (see, e.g., Chen, Roll, and Ross 1986).

split across finer asset classes, such as US, international, and emerging markets for equities and US Treasuries, sovereigns, and corporates for bonds. In this framework, assets are investment vehicles—in practice, they are investment products—that allow investors to "own" a particular set of risk–return exposures, which usually correspond to macro-oriented economic exposures desired by the investor. Thus, in a sense, the "asset-based" approach is actually an "investment product–based" approach.

The factor-based approach is a more modern analytical framework that makes a strong distinction between the investment vehicles themselves and the risk–return exposures that result from owning a particular set of investment vehicles. Under the factor-based approach, rather than assigning weights to assets—which, according to the asset-based approach, indirectly dictates the investor's factor exposures—the investor consciously allocates weights to the factor exposures as a first step and then chooses a collection of assets that yields the target factor exposures. The investor's choice of factor exposures will consider how factors interact with one another and the premiums they generate, whereas the choice of a set of assets that achieves the target factor exposures is typically made on the basis of the valuation level of each of the available assets, with the investor using the most "attractively priced" assets to access the desired factor exposures.[2]

A standard criticism leveled against the traditional asset-based approach is that it leads to portfolios dominated by equity-like risk, even though these portfolios appear to be well diversified.[3] This occurs, at least in part, because very different assets often exhibit strong sensitivity to equity-like risk. Such a critique of asset-based allocation, it

[2]Note that by "unbundling" the decisions on risk and valuation, it is possible to first think carefully about which risks one is willing to take to earn returns and then examine how diversified one's sources of risk are. After answering these questions, investors who believe that assets can be mispriced relative to corresponding risk exposures can pursue asset allocation "alpha" by selecting cheaper assets to gain the desired risk exposures.
[3]The classic pension portfolio, using the 60/40 equity/bond construct, has 90% of its total portfolio variance driven by equity risk. For a review of the risk concentration issue commonly found in asset-based allocation approaches, see Bhansali, Davis, Rennison, Hsu, and Li (2012).

turns out, is both easily understood and readily addressed under the factor-based allocation framework.

Researchers generally recognize a few primary sources of economic risk, including shocks to economic growth, shocks to inflation, and shocks to credit availability. Most assets naturally exhibit multiple economic exposures. Corporate bonds, for example, are exposed to all three of these sources of risk. When there is a significant deterioration in global corporate profitability due to a severe economic downturn, (1) default risk increases as companies become less able to repay their loans, which hurts corporate bond prices, (2) banks and investors are less willing to lend to risky projects, which increases the cost of capital—again, hurting corporate bond prices—and (3) the government benchmark interest rate generally declines as a policy response, which helps bonds of all types. As it happens, high-yield stocks often have significant exposure to exactly these three risks in largely the same fashion. Accordingly, adding corporate bonds to a portfolio of high-yield stocks would not necessarily improve the portfolio's *risk exposure* diversification, despite the increase in *asset class* diversification.

Returning to the diversification-based critique of asset-focused allocation, the problem clearly lies in the order of operations. If one allocates to asset classes in the first step—deciding to invest in corporate bonds and high-yielding stocks, for example—there is no guarantee that the chosen mix of assets will yield a diverse set of factor exposures. Indeed, given the concerns just discussed, chances are it will not. But if one adopts the factor-based approach to allocation, diversified economic exposures can be easily selected in the first step, at which point choosing a specific mix of assets to efficiently achieve the desired factor exposures is all that remains.

2.3. NUTRIENTS ARE TO FOODS AS FACTORS ARE TO ASSETS

Of course, we recognize that the factor-based approach—with its associated technical jargon, such as "factor premiums" and "factor loadings"—can seem unintuitive to many investors. An analogy to food and nutrition may be helpful in this regard.[4] Think of portfolios as meals, assets as food, and factors as nutrients. People need to consume a mixture of nutrients that varies from one person to another on the basis of individual circumstances. Because nutrients come bundled in various foods (e.g., dairy, grains, meats), people must combine foods to create a meal that supplies them with the desired nutrition. However, it is likely that many different meals would provide comparable nutrition. Thus, personal taste and food prices often dictate the preferred meal.

In the language of asset allocation, we note that individual asset classes contain different factor exposures. A desired combination of economic factor exposures can be achieved by different portfolios made up of varying combinations of asset classes. Asset prices, costs, and investment governance will ultimately dictate the preferred portfolio. So, just as the savvy homemaker knows that chicken breasts provide protein more effectively than rib-eye steaks—which are both more expensive and contain more artery-clogging saturated fat—the sophisticated investor recognizes that the master skill is in constructing a portfolio using "attractively priced" asset classes, which provide the desired economic exposures without introducing other unwanted risks.

The analogy to food is also helpful for understanding tactical asset allocation (TAA). When food prices change, we may choose to consume the same nutrients at a lower cost by eating a different meal consisting of different ingredients. If rib-eye steaks go on sale at half price, replacing chicken breasts with steak could be a more efficient route to protein consumption, and the low price might just warrant having a little bit of fat in today's dinner. In the language of factor-based allocation, TAA can be understood as tactically rebalancing toward out-of-favor assets that provide "cheaper" access to a set of underlying economic exposures and away from "expensive" assets offering the same factor exposures.

[4]We did not originate the nutrient–food analogy; it has been used previously by Professor John Cochrane at the University of Chicago and by Professor Andrew Ang at Columbia University.

2.4. APPLICATIONS OF THE RISK-BASED FRAMEWORK

We now illustrate the factor-based framework with four applications, meant to highlight several investment insights that would not be available through traditional asset-based analysis.

APPLICATION 1: RETHINKING "REBALANCING AND THE STRATEGIC PORTFOLIO WEIGHTS"

In the asset-based framework, stocks (proxied by the S&P 500 Index) and bonds (proxied by the BarCap Agg Index) are viewed as fundamental portfolio building blocks.[5] US investors generally hold large, often static strategic allocations tied to the two benchmarks, with a 60% equity/40% bond strategic allocation as the traditional "norm."

It is dangerous, however, to assume that assets like the S&P 500 or the BarCap Agg have static risk exposures over time. In 1995, technology stocks composed 9.4% of the S&P 500. The index had a P/E of 17.4 and a dividend yield of 2.2%. In 2000, technology stocks represented 21.2% of the S&P 500, pushing the index volatility from its historical average of 15% to 24%, the P/E to 24.4, and the dividend yield to 1.2%. Similarly, in 2000, the BarCap Agg had a 4.5-year duration and yielded 6.4%. In Q2 2015, the BarCap Agg had a 5-year duration and an abysmal yield of 1.6%. Clearly, a disciplined rebalance back toward the steady 60/40 allocation over this period would have produced a portfolio with wildly fluctuating underlying risk exposures!

Using the food analogy again, it is instructive to think of the BarCap Agg as a hamburger and the S&P 500 as fruit juice. As America demanded bigger beef patties, fast-food restaurants moved to double patties, often with bacon to boot. The protein levels, not to mention the calories and fat, of today's gourmet burgers are significantly

[5]BarCap Agg is the Barclays Capital Aggregate Bond Index, which is one of the most commonly used bond indexes. It contains almost all the US investment-grade bonds, including Treasury, agency, mortgage, and corporate bonds; the weights are based on the market capitalizations of the bond issues. The index is generally dominated by Treasury bonds owing to the issuance size of US Treasuries relative to other bonds.

higher than those of the burgers of the past (333 calories for an average burger 20 years ago versus 590 calories today). Eating a hamburger today provides a very different set of nutrients versus a decade ago. Similarly, fruit juices today contain more fructose and chemical flavoring than actual fruit juice. It would be unwise to assume that a stable diet of hamburgers and juice provides consistent nutrients over time. A diner consumes more protein and calories in today's burger just as an investor bears more duration risk (interest rate sensitivity risk) in the BarCap Agg today. Likewise, today's juices contain more chemicals (vitamin additives and artificial flavorings) and less fruit, much as today's S&P 500 offers far more tech exposure and far less energy exposure than it did before. Given the Agg's significant increase in duration risk—not to mention its lower yield—is it wise to still insist on a 40% strategic exposure to investment-grade bonds? Without a careful examination of the change in the underlying factor exposures, one may not notice just how wildly one's portfolio has changed over the years even when the asset allocation percentages remain largely similar over the period.

APPLICATION 2: INTERPRETING HEDGE FUND PERFORMANCE

In the asset-based framework, hedge funds are particularly difficult to examine. Many hedge funds trade exotic and illiquid assets. Those that hold conventional securities often apply complex strategies involving leverage and shorting. This complexity has sometimes led investors to treat hedge funds as a separate asset class, to which the cynics retort that the only characteristics shared by members of the hedge fund asset class are opacity and high fees.

Much of this black-box complexity can be unraveled in the factor-based space, providing some useful insights into hedge fund strategies. It turns out that many hedge fund strategies can be mimicked using more liquid and traditional assets, because many hedge funds, despite their exotic holdings and strategies, actually (and probably unintentionally) end up owning fairly commonplace factor exposures. Moreover, for the average fund, there is often little evidence that accessing standard factor exposures through more exotic assets or by using complex trading strategies leads to superior returns.[6] To be fair, some hedge funds do provide exotic return exposures that are not found in conventional assets or strategies. For example, earning returns from exposures to extreme economic shocks by writing options is an innovation that expands the investment frontier.

According to our analogy, hedge fund providers argue that their products offer exclusive nutritional compounds in the form of "alphas" and rare nutrients in the form of "exotic betas." Hard-to-get nutrients and exclusive medicinal herbs are necessarily expensive. However, using factor analysis, much of the hedge fund replication research suggests that the average hedge fund provides nutrients that can be found readily in standard assets; only a small fraction of hedge funds truly provide the hard-to-get "exotic betas," and even fewer provide proprietary "alpha." In this context, most hedge funds are more like foo-foo health foods—bird's nest and shark fin—which, at hundreds to thousands of dollars per pound, are advertised as combating aging and cancer but actually contain nothing more than garden-variety vitamins and proteins. Even for the hedge funds that do provide exotic betas or true alphas, the 2% base fee and 20% performance fee may be so onerous as to make the net-of-cost investment benefit unattractive relative to a portfolio of dumb indexes. Thus, although it could very well be the case that 100-year-old Snow Mountain ginseng improves health in ways that no modern medicine can, at thousands of dollars per 100 grams, this trade-off might be so unappealing that one is better off, healthwise, simply exercising more and working a less stressful day.

APPLICATION 3: RISK PARITY

Risk parity is an asset allocation portfolio heuristic that attempts to provide a diversified portfolio of risk exposures. Specifically, it seeks to overcome the heavy dependence on equities in the conventional 60/40 equity/bond allocation portfolio. As mentioned earlier, the standard criticism against the 60/40 allocation is that the portfolio risk is 90%

[6]See Fung and Hsieh (1997a, 1997b, 2004); Agarwal and Naik (2000); Ennis and Sebastian (2003); Hasanhodzic and Lo (2007). For a comprehensive survey review of the literature on hedge fund performance, see Eling (2008).

driven by equity volatility, such that the asset class allocation percentages grossly misrepresent the actual risk allocation.

Risk parity allocation seeks to address the equity risk concentration issues associated with naive asset-based allocation methods by weighting asset classes using their inverse volatility (i.e., the less volatile asset classes receive more weight). The resulting portfolio is far more diversified in terms of the risk contribution from different asset classes. A risk parity–weighted portfolio of equities and bonds, for example, might result in a 30% allocation to stocks and a 70% allocation to bonds. This 30/70 risk parity portfolio of stocks and bonds does indeed have a higher Sharpe ratio and is more risk diversified than the conventional 60/40 portfolio.

Drilling deeper, however, we see that the implementation of risk parity often occurs in the asset space. This means there will be parity in the assets' contribution to overall portfolio volatility but probably no parity in the underlying economic risk exposures. The popular and standard risk parity solution is based on volatility weighting of "distinct" asset classes. As with a naive reliance on the 60/40 allocation, a naive asset-based approach to risk parity is also suboptimal, because asset classes can often appear distinct but actually contain similar risks.[7] A seemingly diversified risk parity portfolio—constructed from equities, commodities, high-yield credit, real estate, and bonds—is like a mixed grill of beef, pork, lamb, and chicken with a large salad (i.e., not a balanced meal nutritionally). Although the sources of nutrients are diversified, the underlying nutrients are not. Stocks, commodities, credit, and real estate are all procyclical assets, which are sensitive to global growth. Although careful portfolio construction using risk parity might result in equal volatility contributions from these four asset classes, the resulting portfolio would still be overwhelmingly exposed to the growth risk factor. In the long run, sadly, this risk parity portfolio probably provides no better diversification than a simple 60/40 equity/bond portfolio. Both would be dominated by the global growth risk factor, with little exposure to other important factors.

[7]See Chaves, Hsu, Li, and Shakernia (2012); Bhansali et al. (2012).

Thus, a risk parity approach would be more appropriate and consistent with its original intent if applied in the factor domain rather than the asset class domain.

APPLICATION 4: ESG

A central question in ESG (environmental, social, and governance) investing is whether ESG screens and overlays hurt portfolio returns. From an asset class perspective, it is difficult to answer this question. ESG can easily alter the composition of assets by meaningfully changing the country and sector allocation of a portfolio. These deviations can often be substantial. From the traditional asset allocation perspective, the large changes in country and sector weights seem to imply a meaningful impact on portfolio risk and return, although the quantitative magnitude and even direction remain unclear. Would underweighting the beverage (alcohol) industry, for example, reduce returns or reduce portfolio diversification negatively and meaningfully in the long run? It would be impossible to answer that question without a crystal ball to reveal the long-term returns of the beverage industry versus other industries.

Active portfolio managers argue that ESG restrictions must necessarily reduce portfolio returns because they constrain the manager's opportunity set and thus hinder the manager's ability to generate alpha. Although this might be true, the alpha impact is likely secondary, if not tertiary, which is clearer when considered under a factor-based framework. According to factor-based portfolio analysis, the return of a portfolio is driven in part by factor exposures and in part by the true alpha associated with active management. This framework allows us to examine a manager's alpha contribution very simply by using empirical analysis. The data from the last three decades suggest that, globally, the true alpha component is largely zero to negative, net of fees. As a result, it is not clear that constraining the average manager from fully expressing her investment views would be particularly performance reducing.

If ESG is to have a meaningful impact, then, it must come from its influence on the underlying allocation across factor exposures. Do industries that tend to score poorly on ESG (e.g., gaming, alcohol, and military) have very different factor exposures relative to other industries? Again, an empirical analysis using the factor framework could resolve this question much more readily and with greater reliability than the traditional asset class approach. Note that the traditional asset-based approach would probably call for a simple comparison of the historical returns of non-ESG-favorable industries with those of other industries—a method that, owing to its low statistical power, unfortunately offers almost no information.

As it turns out, there are more industries and countries than there are meaningful factors that drive portfolio returns. Accordingly, the factor framework suggests that even if an ESG screen changes a portfolio's country and industry mix, it need not change the portfolio's factor exposures. The underweight in alcohol called for by a new ESG program, for instance, could be combined with an overweight in other consumer cyclicals to maintain largely the same portfolio factor exposures and desired long-term risk–return profile. Simply put, if one decides to become a vegetarian and can no longer eat meat, one can simply replace animal-based protein with a plant-based protein source. Although the meals might look very different, the mix of nutrients will remain largely similar.

2.5. CAUTIONARY NOTES

UNDERSTANDING DIFFERENT CATEGORIES OF FACTOR EXPOSURES

Factor terminology, unfortunately, is frequently used imprecisely—sometimes altogether incorrectly. It is worthwhile to review some of the nuances that are often glossed over, leading to confusion and misunderstanding. There are essentially three types of factor exposures (for a careful statistical treatment of this topic, see Pukthuanthong and Roll 2014):

1. Those that appear uncorrelated with economic risk exposures yet generate excess returns
2. Those that are correlated with macro risks and thus produce excess returns

3. Those that seem to be correlated with sources of risk but do not give rise to excess returns

It should be clear that investing in portfolios that provide a return premium without exposure to economic risks is very desirable. Generally, factors that provide this seemingly anomalous return premium are referred to as "behavioral" factors. Many financial economists have argued that the value factor and the momentum factor are behavioral factors because they do not seem to be correlated with such macroeconomic risk exposures as global growth, liquidity, inflation, and geopolitical stability. Of course, one should not naively interpret these behavioral exposures as a "free lunch." The anomalous premiums associated with such exposures persist precisely because holding these behavioral exposures is psychologically uncomfortable, even if doing so causes no long-term physical harm to investor wealth. The psychology literature has taught us that the unhappiness caused by imagined harm is no different from the unhappiness arising from actual harm. Investing in a value strategy (or contrarian investing, in general) might thus be compared to a child eating broccoli. Although it might result in a better portfolio outcome in the long run, the psychological trauma in the short run could be so large as to not be worthwhile.

Factor exposures that correlate with economic risks are the easiest to comprehend. The return premium associated with the exposure is compensation for bearing risk. These exposures, as mentioned earlier, are the proteins, carbohydrates, fats, and vitamins needed for a healthy body.

There are also factor exposures that correlate with other sources of risk but offer no appreciable premium to speak of. These exposures are clearly undesirable in a portfolio and often correspond to large idiosyncratic risks, such as idiosyncratic company distress or industry risk. Think of these as foods without much nutritional content: so-called empty calories. Because foods with useful nutrients already provide ample calories, eating foods with empty calories—think desserts and sugary snacks—is unwise. They cost money and put stress on your body to process but offer no appreciable benefits.

THE ROLE OF PRICE IN FACTOR-BASED PORTFOLIO ALLOCATION

The beauty of the food analogy is that it illustrates the power of the factor framework to help investors make better allocations as well as the dangers associated with a narrow focus on factor investing while ignoring asset classes. The factor framework tells us that whether we invest in US, European, Japanese, or Chinese equities, we are exposed to the global growth factor and earn the risk premium associated with that exposure. This is similar to the recognition that whether we eat a steak, a duck breast, or a salmon fillet—seemingly very different meals—we are nonetheless consuming protein. Although the tastes of these meals might be very different, we would be fooling ourselves if we failed to acknowledge that these meals are nutritionally quite similar and would not come together to create a balanced diet, because they are lacking in things like fiber, carbohydrates, and vitamin C. The factor framework helps us understand more scientifically the portfolio diversification that is not obvious when viewed from the asset perspective.

It is worth noting that there is a useful intuition around "price" that is often omitted by proponents of the factor-based framework for portfolio allocation. Many supporters of the factor framework also happen to be strong believers in market efficiency. Thus, the factor perspective often comes with no sense of valuation—nothing is either expensive or cheap. Under this worldview, there are no behavioral factors that offer returns without corresponding risks; two portfolios consisting of different asset mixes with very different valuations (in absolute or relative terms) but having the same factor exposures, as measured by the portfolios' return sensitivities to various risk factors, would be deemed to offer the same risk–return profile in the long run. Price clearly plays no role in this particular interpretation of factor-based portfolio allocation.

Indeed, we think it is dangerous to assume that factor loadings are the only salient pieces of information relevant to investors' decisions or to treat portfolios with similar factor exposures as largely identical, irrespective of the prices at which they trade. A range of asset combinations can result in similar factor exposures, just as a large variety of foods can be combined to create different meals providing similar nutrients. Although a chef might care deeply about the nutrients in the meals she consumes, she probably cares just as much about the cost of the ingredients that go into her dishes. If salmon is on sale at the supermarket, the chef is likely to prepare a meal based on salmon. To clarify, we do not advocate that investors favor one factor exposure over another simply because it is cheaper by some valuation measure. Protein is more expensive than carbohydrates, but one would not replace protein with carbs on the basis of price alone. We argue that similar proteins sell for very different prices at different points in time and at different locations. Chicken breast might be cheaper than pork right now; Japanese Wagyu beef is meaningfully more expensive than US grain-fed beef. Such information will naturally factor into one's choice of meal.

It is important to remember that investors *transact* in the asset space and that there are often a dozen different asset mixes that provide exposure to the same factor. The successful investor will buy his factor exposures cheaply. Suppose that one can buy global growth by purchasing either emerging-market stocks or US stocks. If emerging-market stocks have a cyclically adjusted P/E (CAPE) of around 12 and US stocks' P/E is around 25, should it not matter whether we purchase global growth through emerging-market equities or US equities?

AVOID GOING TOO FAR WITH THE FACTOR-BASED APPROACH

Finally, we caution against the emerging trend toward "pure" factor portfolios. Going back to the food–nutrient analogy, would we consider it wise to replace traditional home-cooked meals with a chemical cocktail of vitamins and nutritional supplements? Similarly, should we expect factor portfolios constructed from long–short portfolios on the basis of complex quantitative models to provide more effective and complete access to the essential drivers of long-term returns than traditional long-only mainstream asset classes? As researchers who have observed firsthand how little we actually know and how much of what we thought we knew turns out to be wrong as we learn more, we generally fear the extremeness and definitiveness associated with optimized and overengineered solutions. The certainty that often comes from financial engineering can feel like hubris, and we suspect that hubris overestimates the current state of our knowledge—regarding both nutritional health and economics.

Practically speaking, the lay boards of large pension funds and the patriarchs of family offices are unlikely to be familiar with the factor framework and its nomenclature. Therefore, skilled and effective portfolio allocators must always communicate using the language of the asset-based approach. Our desire may be to help our clients consume a balanced diet of all the essential nutrients in the appropriate amounts, but we are likely to be more successful when offering dietary guidance on such familiar meals as steak, fish, pasta, salads, sautéed vegetables, and rice.

2.6. CONCLUSION

When investors analyze choices in the asset-based framework, the large variety of different yet related assets can make the analysis extremely complex; naive investors can often mistake the asset diversity in their portfolios for adequate risk diversification. Further, because the standard view of assets bundles notions of risk and valuation, analysis would be easier if we unpacked the two components, dealing with them in sequence. We have demonstrated that the factor-based approach to asset allocation allows us to separate the two, leading to more intuitive and perhaps more sensible portfolio solutions. Despite the technical jargon and the seemingly abstract framework, the factor-based approach has a great deal to offer investors—particularly in a world where investment options and strategies are becoming exponentially more complex.

REFERENCES

Agarwal, Vikas, and Narayan Y. Naik. 2000. "Multi-Period Performance Persistence Analysis of Hedge Funds." *Journal of Financial and Quantitative Analysis*, vol. 35, no. 3 (September): 327–342.

Bhansali, Vineer, Josh Davis, Graham Rennison, Jason Hsu, and Feifei Li. 2012. "The Risk in Risk Parity: A Factor-Based Analysis of Asset-Based Risk Parity." *Journal of Investing*, vol. 21, no. 3 (Fall): 102–110.

Chaves, Denis, Jason Hsu, Feifei Li, and Omid Shakernia. 2012. "Efficient Algorithms for Computing Risk Parity Portfolio Weights." *Journal of Investing*, vol. 21, no. 3 (Fall): 150–163.

Chen, Nai-Fu, Richard Roll, and Stephen Ross. 1986. "Economic Forces and the Stock Market." *Journal of Business*, vol. 59, no. 3 (July): 383–403.

Eling, Martin. 2008. "Does Hedge Fund Performance Persist? Overview and New Empirical Evidence." Working Paper 37, University of St. Gallen Law & Economics Series.

Ennis, Richard M., and Michael D. Sebastian. 2003. "A Critical Look at the Case for Hedge Funds." *Journal of Portfolio Management*, vol. 29, no. 4 (Summer): 103–112.

Fung, William, and David A. Hsieh. 1997a. "Empirical Characteristics of Dynamic Trading Strategies: The Case of Hedge Funds." *Review of Financial Studies*, vol. 10, no. 2 (Summer): 275–302.

———. 1997b. "Survivorship Bias and Investment Style in the Returns of CTAs." *Journal of Portfolio Management*, vol. 24, no. 1 (Fall): 30–41.

———. 2004. "Hedge Fund Benchmarks: A Risk-Based Approach." *Financial Analysts Journal*, vol. 60, no. 5 (September/October): 65–80.

Hasanhodzic, Jasmina, and Andrew W. Lo. 2007. "Can Hedge-Fund Returns Be Replicated?: The Linear Case." *Journal of Investment Management*, vol. 5, no. 2 (Second Quarter): 5–45.

Pukthuanthong, Kuntara, and Richard Roll. 2014. "A Protocol for Factor Identification." Working paper.

Ross, Stephen. 1976. "The Arbitrage Theory of Capital Asset Pricing," *Journal of Economic Theory*, vol. 13, no. 3 (December): 341–360.

3. DYNAMIC ASSET ALLOCATION: GREAT EXPECTATIONS

Brian D. Singer, CFA

> Out into the deep of the great dark world,
> Beyond the long borders where foam and drift
> Of the sundering wave are lost and gone
> On the tides that plunge and rear and crumble.
>
> —*Carl Sandburg, "From the Shore"*[1]

Below the ocean's surface, individual fish swim in schools of collective behavior. From above, the tides, the waves, and especially the ripples reflect and distort both the aquatic environment below and the terrestrial surroundings above. This singular system seems quite different from each perspective. Similarly, investment professionals scrutinize the global capital markets from above and below. Top-down investors seek to ride macrothematic tides, navigate intervening waves, and ignore distracting ripples. Conversely, bottom-up analysts endeavor to benefit from unique insights into individual company characteristics and prospects. Over time, the distinction between top-down and bottom-up has blurred; investors increasingly comprehend that many things transpiring below the surface are wrought by the ebbs and flows of tides and waves. Asset allocation, in its many forms, is the discipline of exploiting evidence discernible at the ocean's surface.

3.1. AN ARRAY OF ASSET ALLOCATION STRATEGIES

Over the years, there has been much debate over the percentage of return and return variation attributable to asset allocation. The seminal work was written by Gary Brinson and Nimrod Fachler to "propose

[1]Carl Sandburg, "From the Shore," in *Chicago Poems* (New York: Henry Holt, 1916): www.bartleby.com/165/.

an analytical framework for evaluating the portfolio's performance."[2] Subsequent research by Brinson and others, using this framework, found that the investment *policy* benchmark explains about 90% of the *variation* in quarterly returns.[3]

More recently, Roger Ibbotson and Paul Kaplan explored attribution from several angles, providing greater insight.[4] They concluded that "about 90 percent of the variability in returns of a typical fund *across time* is explained by policy, about 40 percent of the variation of returns among funds [*across funds*] is explained by policy and on average about 100 percent of the return *level* is explained by the policy return level." The first conclusion corroborates the conclusion of Brinson and others. The second conclusion contributes to the existing body of knowledge by using a larger database to address performance variation across funds. The last conclusion is a gross-of-fee tautology when studying large numbers of funds.

Despite the capital market characteristics that these studies confirm, relatively limited resources and primitive tools often direct asset allocations. The early Brinson and more recent Ibbotson studies' conclusions pertain to *policy asset allocations*. Given that the policy asset allocation drives 90% of the return variation *over time* and 40% *across funds*, asset owners can reasonably expect to steer their portfolio outcomes toward long-term goals by establishing policy asset allocations. These policy allocations are based on equilibrium expected returns and risks of all policy-encompassed asset classes. Equilibrium expected returns are those that provide a real risk-free return and an inflation premium available to all asset classes and risk premiums unique to each asset class. The risk premiums are derived from the nondiversifiable risk

---

[2]Gary P. Brinson and Nimrod Fachler, "Measuring Non-U.S. Equity Portfolio Performance," *Journal of Portfolio Management*, vol. 11, no. 3 (Spring 1985): 73–76.

[3]Gary P. Brinson, L. Randolph Hood, and Gilbert L. Beebower, "Determinants of Portfolio Performance," *Financial Analysts Journal*, vol. 42, no. 4 (July/August 1986): 39–44; Gary P. Brinson, Brian D. Singer, and Gilbert L. Beebower, "Determinants of Portfolio Performance II: An Update," *Financial Analysts Journal*, vol. 47, no. 3 (May/June 1991): 40–48.

[4]Roger G. Ibbotson and Paul D. Kaplan, "Does Asset Allocation Policy Explain 40, 90, or 100 Percent of Performance?" *Financial Analysts Journal*, vol. 56, no. 1 (January/February 2000): 26–33.

embedded in an equilibrium covariance matrix. Thus, the equilibrium covariance matrix serves two purposes: to determine all asset class risk premiums and the risks needed to determine an efficient policy asset allocation.

A typical policy asset allocation includes some delineation of traditional asset classes, such as global equities and bonds; nontraditional assets, such as private equity, real estate, timber, and infrastructure; and strategies, such as hedge funds. These can be further segmented into market, sector, emerging, investment grade, high yield inflation linked, distinct types of private equity, and a variety of hedge fund strategies.

Many asset owners prefer to use *strategic asset allocations* (SAAs) that are slightly more flexible than their policy allocations. An SAA deviates from the invariant policy allocation for a period of time that is long but not as long as the policy horizon. Occasionally, say, annually or every few years, the asset owner makes a strategic tilt to the policy allocation to capture perceived capital market opportunities. Subsequent investment strategies are made relative to the SAA, as if it were the policy allocation. The SAA typically comprises small tilts away from the policy such that the portfolio remains aligned with the specific objectives and constraints that determine the policy mix.

In the early 1950s, Harry Markowitz and Bill Sharpe opened investors' eyes to and provided the theory for fund diversification. Their modern portfolio theory (MPT) not only guided policy allocations but also facilitated the development of rudimentary tools to affect efficient portfolios as circumstances changed. *Dynamic asset allocation* (DAA) and *tactical asset allocation* (TAA) emerged to help navigate these changes. DAA is longer term than TAA in its application.

DAA is built on the concept of intrinsic (or fundamental) value, a concept that was pioneered by Benjamin Graham early in the 20th century. In *Security Analysis*, Graham and his co-author, David Dodd, stated that an analyst's concern is "with the intrinsic value of the security and more particularly with the discovery of discrepancies between the intrinsic value and the market price."[5] Further, they described speculative factors that influence price "through the intermediary of people's sentiments and decisions."[6]

In today's parlance, intrinsic value is the present value of expected future cash flows discounted by an interest rate that reflects nondiversifiable risk. The long-term fundamentally determined intrinsic value of either an individual security or an index of such securities can be determined in this manner. According to Gary Brinson, DAA[7] "means deviating temporarily from the normal policy mix. It is based upon judgments that one or more asset classes is in a state of disequilibrium with respect to the investment characteristics that were utilized in forming the policy mix."[8]

DAA is a fundamentally driven, intermediate-term approach that rides the tide of discrepancies between intrinsic values and market prices. Intrinsic values exert a "gravitational" pull on asset and index prices that inexorably drives them toward equilibrium. An index's price temporarily varies around, but is always drawn toward, its intrinsic value, as shown in **Exhibit 3.1**.

A dynamic asset allocator's job would be relatively easy if prices converged on intrinsic values overnight; however, investors must abide reality. Because convergence does not occur overnight, investors must navigate the waves that jostle and potentially capsize their portfolio boats. Index prices' deviations from intrinsic values have half-lives of about four years and can be said to substantially converge over an 8- to 10-year period.[9]

---

[5]Benjamin Graham and David L. Dodd, *Security Analysis: Principles and Technique*, 6th ed. (New York: McGraw-Hill, 2009): 64.
[6]Graham and Dodd, *Security Analysis*, 70.
[7]At the time of authorship, Brinson simply referred to "dynamic asset allocation" as "asset allocation." The only distinctions were policy and asset allocations.
[8]Gary P. Brinson, "Asset Allocation vs. Market Timing," *Investment Management Review* (September/October 1988).
[9]The half-life indicates how long it takes for half of the value/price discrepancy to close.

EXHIBIT 3.1. PRICE VARIATION AS IT CONVERGES ON INTRINSIC VALUE

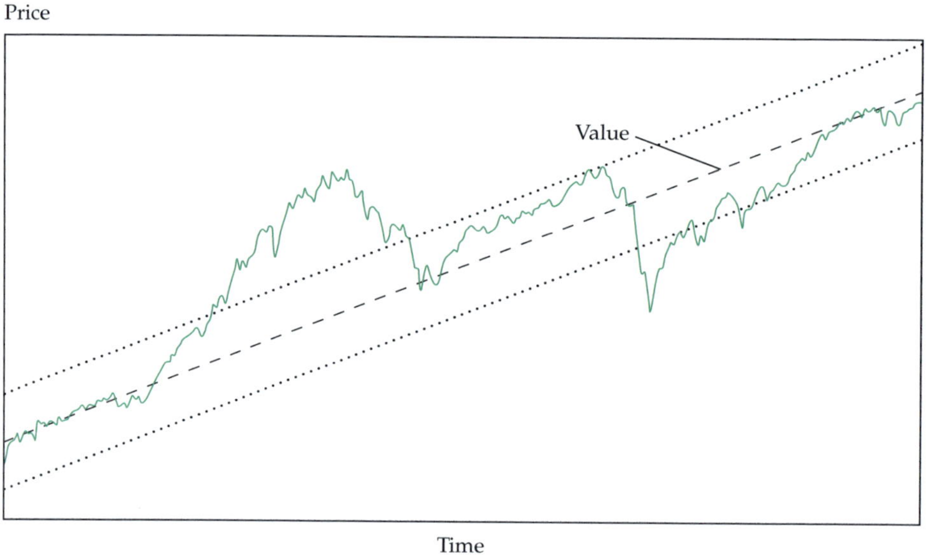

Source: William Blair.

Brinson distinguishes tactical asset allocation (TAA) by describing market timing as "the alteration of an asset mix motivated by a forecast of future price change."[10] Considering shorter-term horizons, market timing references *global tactical asset allocation* (GTAA) and its domestic sister, TAA. Price movement *forecasts* are typically for relatively short horizons and are predicated on the analysis of past prices or underlying macroeconomic and geopolitical developments and such ratios as price to book, and market behavior or mass psychology. Whether one uses a technical analysis of price patterns or price momentum or a top-down fundamental analysis, the objective is to *forecast* future market price direction and magnitude.

To John Maynard Keynes, speculation was the forecasting of market psychology. From this perspective, GTAA and TAA

[10]Brinson, "Asset Allocation vs. Market Timing."

> are, in fact, largely concerned, not with making superior long-term forecasts of the probable yield of an investment over its life, but with forecasting changes in the conventional basis of valuation a short time ahead of the general public. They are concerned, not with what an investment is really worth to a man who buys it "for keeps," but with what the market will value it at, under the influence of mass psychology, three months to a year hence. Moreover, this behaviour is not the outcome of wrong-headed propensity. . . . For it is not sensible to pay 25 for an investment of which you believe the prospective yield to justify a value of 30, if you also believe that the market will value it at 20 three months hence.[11]

The "speculation" that Keynes referred to provides liquidity to capital markets, facilitating the continual process of price discovery such that scarce capital is directed to attractive investment opportunities. Myriad buyers and sellers with different time horizons, objectives, and constraints determine the evolution of price over time. At one end of the spectrum, a short-horizon investor, such as a market maker or high-frequency trader, continually transacts on the basis of time-proximate information. Alternatively, a long-horizon investor occasionally transacts when price deviates from future cash flow value. In between, day traders, quantitative and discretionary investors, and others converge on the market in pursuit of their own unique objectives. In this manner, price equilibrates the instantaneous supply of and demand for capital. Each market participant's actions stem from disparately known and uniquely valued information. This chaotic sequential short-term behavior pushes prices around but slowly and inexorably toward long-term intrinsic values. If price deviates from intrinsic value too much, longer-horizon investors will step in to take advantage of information and knowledge valuable to them but not necessarily relevant to short-term investors.

---

[11]John M. Keynes, *The General Theory of Employment, Interest and Money* (New York: Harcourt Brace Jovanovich, 1964): 154–155.

After the Cold War and the subsequent period of US hegemony, "mutually assured destruction" has been replaced with geopolitical uncertainty and populist and other macrothematic waves. It is not sensible to ignore "the influence of mass psychology" that arises with the evolving uncertainties observed since about 2000.

3.2. SYSTEMATIC RISK ALLOCATION

Asset allocation is now just one segment of a growing top-down universe that not only is more granular than before but also encompasses other systematic investment processes. Top-down investors allocate funds across compensated systematic risks. Historically, these systematic risks were proxied by asset classifications of similar characteristics, such as fixed or variable cash flows, and by organizational structures, such as domestic or international analysts. Top-down investing has involved shifting among these systematic asset class risk buckets by changing asset class, or "traditional beta," allocations. Seeking competitive advantage, top-down investors have pursued greater risk granularity across markets, sectors, credits, and currencies. But this could progress only so far. Now, highly competitive investors are pushing beyond these static groupings to identify and gain access to additional exploitable, systematically compensated behaviors and risks. Analytic sophistication has advanced beyond single-period MPT constructs—narrower than the long-term tidal pull of value—and analyzing short- and intermediate-term investor behavior and risk factor waves.

How much capital market return variance is due to systematic factors? If there were none other than market risk, then these top-down endeavors would be for naught. If significant, then the top-down search for systematic risk factors would be of value.

Staub and Singer hypothesized that capital market returns are determined by multiple systematic risks (multiple betas) and concluded that systematic, or macro, decisions explain nearly twice the idiosyncratic security contribution. With respect to typical capital market characteristics, "independent of any perception of how a portfolio should be structured," two-thirds of a portfolio's return variation over time is due to asset allocation (systematic risk exposures) and one-third to security selection.[12] This conclusion is based on the analysis of a universe of 20 national equity markets and 20 national bond markets, where each market includes 100 securities. If all securities were perfectly correlated, the only practical decision would be an asset/cash decision. With more realistic assumptions that allow partial security independence, security selection explains 35% of return variation and 65% is the result of systematic risks:

- Stocks in a national market have a correlation of 0.50.
- Bonds in a national market have a correlation of 0.80.
- Stocks of different national markets have a correlation of 0.40.
- Bonds of different national markets have a correlation of 0.60.
- Stocks and bonds of the same national market have a correlation of 0.30.
- Stocks and bonds of different national markets have a correlation of 0.20.

Asset management has long been characterized as either "traditional" or "alternative." The exploitation of systematic risks, previously the realm of hedge funds, has spawned part of an entirely new type of asset management vehicle referred to as "liquid alternatives."

Traditional portfolios are built on strategic policy allocations or capitalization-weighted benchmarks. Such long-only portfolios derive most of their performance from broad market exposure and because they are managed relative to benchmarks and have limited the scope of performance contributions from security and asset class weight variation.

[12]Renato Staub and Brian D. Singer, "Asset Allocation vs. Security Selection: Their Relative Importance," *CFA Institute Investment Performance Measurement Feature Articles*, vol. 2011, no. 1 (May 2011): 7.

Alternative portfolios relax the traditional constraints and attempt to deviate from easily and cheaply attainable market risk to create uncorrelated return streams.

More recently, however, investors have realized that many alternative investments are capturing systematic opportunities that can be replicated at much lower cost and with considerably more liquidity. These "liquid alternatives" straddle the traditional and alternative divide, drawing on the better features of each world—the liquidity and low fees of traditional portfolios and the flexibility of alternative portfolios.

Because the liquid alternative phenomenon is relatively recent, a standard nomenclature has yet to fully emerge, and so such phrases as "liquid alternatives," "smart beta," and "alternative beta" are loosely used. The emerging investment management paradigm may be made clearer by providing an investment taxonomy delineating and specifying nomenclature for many methods of investment management. Other taxonomies could be crafted, but this captures the current state of the industry in a manner that best identifies the new and growing liquid alternative investment approach.

3.3. INVESTMENT TAXONOMY AND LIQUID ALTERNATIVES

As shown in **Exhibit 3.2**, the primary branches are liquid and illiquid investments. The liquid investments are separated into traditional and alternative investments. Of course, illiquid investments can be similarly split, but this representation focuses on only the liquid branch. *Traditional* liquid investments comprise long-only portfolios that are either actively or passively managed relative to a specified market-cap benchmark, SAA, or policy asset allocation.

Liquid alternative investment approaches—typically referred to as "liquid alts"—capture underlying systematic risk factors, many of which had previously been exploitable only by hedge funds. In some instances, liquid alts are specifically designed to replicate one or more

EXHIBIT 3.2. INVESTMENT TAXONOMY AND LIQUID ALTERNATIVES

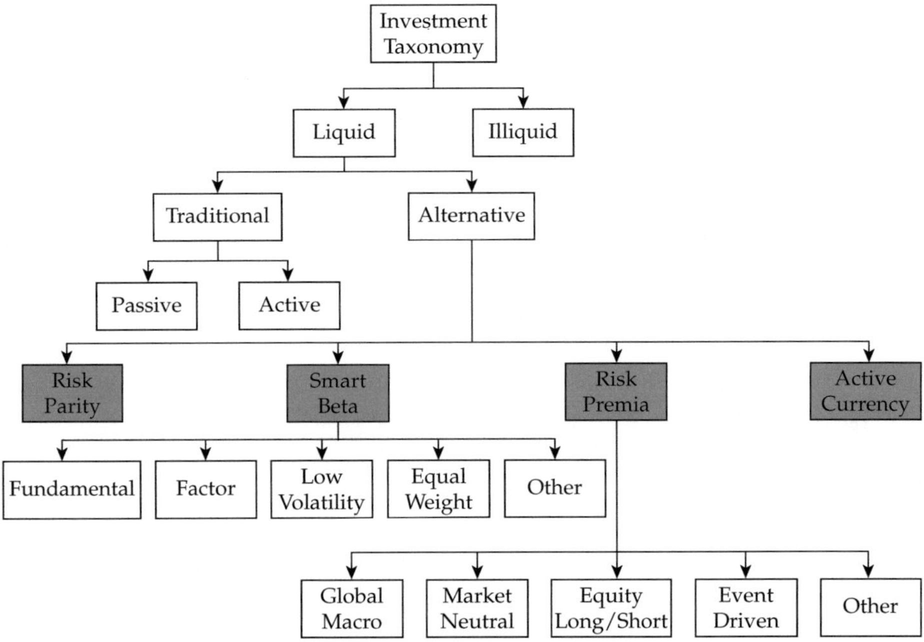

Source: William Blair.

hedge fund categories. Consequently, using such strategies introduces liquid risk factor diversification into portfolios.

There are four primary liquid alt categories: risk parity, smart beta, risk premium, and currency. *Risk parity* portfolios are built on the premise that a portfolio should distribute risk exposures evenly across assets and commodities. If risks were equally distributed across all risk categories, the risk parity approach would build the global capital market portfolio. Thus, its foundation is solid and actual results depend on active deviations from the market portfolio. In practice, the market portfolio is not the objective of any risk parity portfolio. The more qualitative approach, pioneered by Ray Dalio at Bridgewater, distributes its risks in a manner that balances growth and inflation risks and is designed to perform well in all environments.[13] Quantitative approaches balance risk exposures to equities, bonds, and commodities to limit the portfolio swings due simply (and primarily) to equity market risk exposure. Risks are derived from historical data, and portfolios are rebalanced regularly.

Smart beta portfolios are rules-based strategies that effectively build indexes that are not market-cap weighted. These strategies are all thought to have risk and return characteristics that are superior to those of market-cap-based indexes. Some capture underlying compensated risk factors and others replicate systematic elements of hedge funds. Because systematic exposures can be replicated cheaply, smart beta has disrupted some hedge fund strategies at near-passive fee levels. In addition to being low fee, these strategies are liquid, transparent, and mechanically constructed on the basis of prespecified rule sets. They merely require ongoing rebalancing to maintain compliance with the rule set.

As shown in **Exhibit 3.3**, the emergence of smart beta further narrows what can viably be classified as alpha. Because many smart beta strategies pursue persistent and systematic risk exposures—with market risk being the largest—they add betas to the market portfolio beta and leave less to be categorized as pure alpha.

Among smart beta approaches are fundamental indexation and factor, equal weight, and low volatility strategies. Fundamental indexation was popularized by Rob Arnott's 2005 introduction of the Research Affiliates Fundamental Index (RAFI). Fundamental indexes are predicated on fundamental information, such as dividends, cash flow, sales, and price-to-book ratios. Any number of fundamental measures can be used to specify the rules for construction of a fundamental index.

Factor strategies are not new, but they have grown explosively since the mid-1990s. They attempt to identify compensated systematic risk

[13]Matthew C. Klein, "Bridgewater's 'All Weather' Strategy Aims to Balance Risk across Economic Environments: Myths and Facts about 'Risk Parity,'" *Financial Times* (25 August 2015).

EXHIBIT 3.3. IS SYSTEMATIZED ALPHA—"SMART BETA"—A FREE LUNCH?

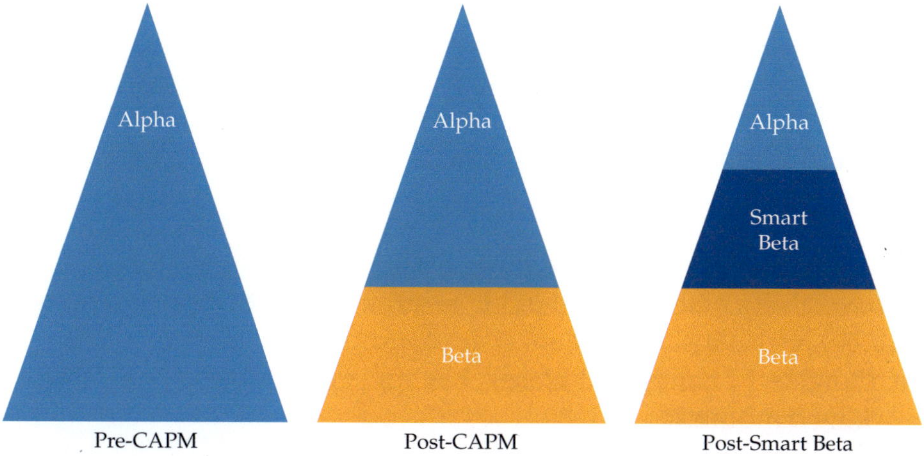

Source: William Blair.

factors, or "alternative betas," and build portfolios accordingly. The first incarnation of a factor-based strategy was originated theoretically by Stephen Ross in 1976 and was empirically tested in 1980.[14] The approach became widely practiced after Fama and French empirically confirmed that three factors—market, size, and book-to-market ratio—capture a significant amount of cross-sectional variation in average stock returns.[15] Mark Carhart subsequently added momentum as a fourth factor, and the four-factor model became an equity hedge fund favorite.[16] Since then, the alternative beta set has expanded to include value, inflation, currency, carry, and credit, among others. The alternative risk premiums that had been the purview of hedge funds have become available in low-fee liquid strategies open to the public, enabling macro risk exposure diversification.

[14]Stephen Ross, "The Arbitrage Theory of Capital Asset Pricing," *Journal of Economic Theory*, vol. 13, no. 3 (December 1976): 341–360; Richard Roll and Stephen Ross, "An Empirical Investigation of the Arbitrage Pricing Theory," *Journal of Finance*, vol. 35, no. 5 (December 1980): 1073–1103.

[15]Eugene F. Fama and Kenneth R. French, "The Cross-Section of Expected Stock Returns," *Journal of Finance*, vol. 47, no. 2 (June 1992): 427–465.

[16]Mark M. Carhart, "On Persistence in Mutual Fund Performance," *Journal of Finance*, vol. 52, no. 1 (March 1997): 57–82.

Equal-weight strategies avoid the higher-priced securities (or asset classes) that may be bubble-priced in market-cap portfolios. Even if not dictated by pricing extremes, market-cap strategies induce the behavior of buying high and selling low. The earliest application of an alternatively weighted index seeking to avoid market-cap pitfalls that I can recall is the GDP-weighted index created by MSCI in 1988, which served to bring the weight of Japan down from 41% to 19% not long before that market's 61% decline from December 1989 to August 1992.

Low-volatility strategies are designed to exploit the systematic low beta/volatility market comparable returns with a lower risk than traditional portfolios. *Ex post* analysis suggests that the compensation is attributable to behavioral biases, but no explanation is more than a working hypothesis.

The crucial feature of smart beta strategies is that they are rules based and, therefore, passive. Consequently, they lend themselves to exchange-traded fund (ETF) implementation. But the strategies considered part of the *risk premium* category are actively managed. Risk premium strategies are total return (not necessarily market neutral) oriented and rely on active long–short investing in liquid securities or instruments. Again, the nature of risk premium strategies effects transparency and relatively low fees. Furthering the risk factor diversification provided by risk parity and smart beta strategies, the risk premium branch includes global macro, long–short equity, market-neutral, and event-driven strategies. Because they are actively managed, little can be said about how each type is managed; however, macro strategies invest in securities and aggregates in equity and bond markets and currencies around the world. The others are self-descriptive.

3.4. HIDDEN DIVERSITY IN ACTIVE CURRENCY

Active currency, the last liquid alt in our investment taxonomy, can do a lot of the "heavy lifting" in DAA. The primary objective of investors in active top-down capabilities is positive real returns without the downside of equities when markets experience a protracted downside. Dynamic management of currency exposures separate from market exposures is getting more attention against a backdrop of low expected returns, divergent and extreme central bank policies, and the need for diversification.

It is common to find technical or systematic currency portfolio managers. Most use straightforward carry and momentum strategies, with differences driven mostly by implementation. Fundamental currency management is much less common. Consistent with the fundamental DAA framework, "value" in the context of exchange rates (relative prices) is not a discounted-cash-flow concept in the way it is for assets or indexes but, rather, a framework of relative purchasing power parity and persistent differences in carry, or real cash rates. There is ill-founded skepticism in the marketplace that exchange rates converge to intrinsic values over the medium term, yet both the theoretical underpinning and the empirical evidence indicate that currencies do, in fact, revert to equilibrium exchange rates and do so with greater robustness than is the case for equities or bonds. The theory can be appreciated by considering that although the expected cash flows arising from asset claims—and the discount rates that should be applied to these flows—are not directly observable and need to be estimated under conditions of uncertainty, the relative prices of goods and services in common currency terms across national borders are much more visible. From a McDonald's "Big Mac" (popularized by the *Economist*'s somewhat frivolous yet informative index of currency valuation) to baskets of internationally traded items represented by producer price baskets recorded in national statistical data, misalignments in purchasing power are apparent. Empirically, it can be shown that for a range of currencies, prices have reverted to straightforward measures of exchange rate equilibria over a shorter time window than intrinsic value reversion for markets, as shown in **Exhibit 3.4**.[17] Currencies and equities each reflect a wide range of convergence periods. The averages indicate that the equity 3.3 year convergence half-life is higher than 2.8 years for currencies. While it is inappropriate to excise extreme events, the Asian currency crisis elevated the convergence half-lives of SGD, KRW, and THB. Absent these currencies and PHP to cover all affected Asian currencies, the

[17]William Blair, "Currency Management: The Case for Value Investing," white paper (November 2014, updated in 2017).

EXHIBIT 3.4. AVERAGE HALF-LIFE OF CURRENCY AND ASSET REVERSION OF PRICE TO VALUE (YEARS)

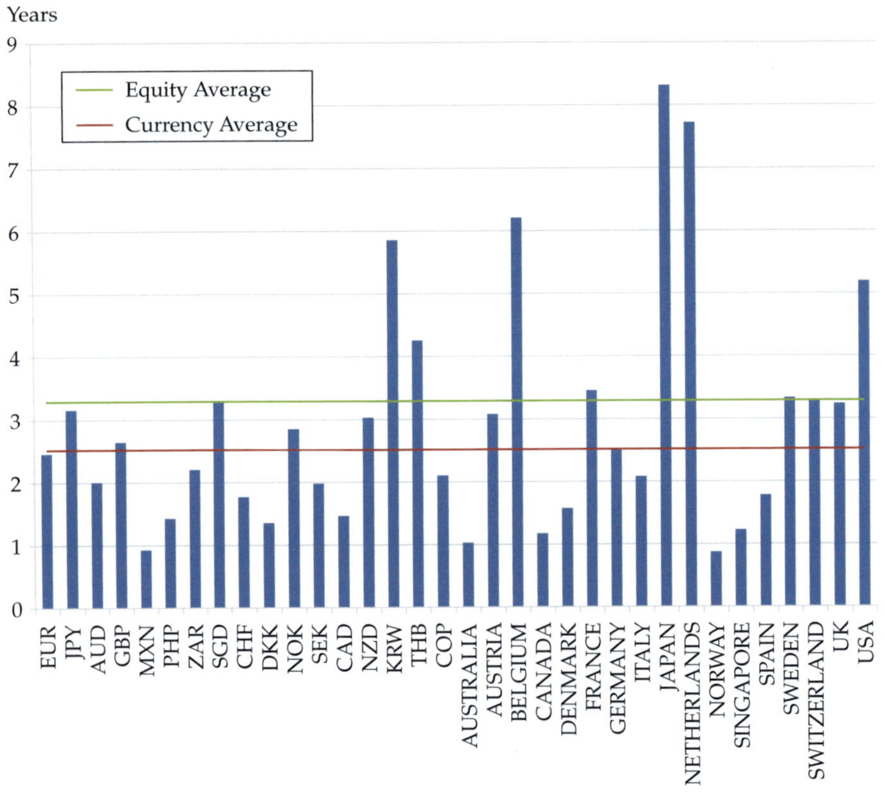

Source: William Blair.

currency half-life would drop to two years. Qualitatively, the currency and equity half-lives would be about 2.5 and 3.3 years.

The second valuable feature is diversification. Exchange rates have very low correlations with equities and bonds over time. Theoretically, their correlation is zero, because currencies do not have risk premiums and are not claims on underlying economic wealth generation. In practice, correlations are sometimes positive (e.g., the positive correlation that was observed between "commodity-sensitive" currencies and their associated equity markets during the steep falls in commodity prices in 2015) but are also sometimes negative (such as the response of the euro, which depreciated, compared with that of eurozone equities, which rallied, during the early stages of the European Central Bank's quantitative easing announcements in 2014).

The diversification potential is demonstrated by a scatterplot of monthly USD Index and MSCI World USD-hedged index returns.[18] The hedged MSCI is unaffected directly by each constituent's currency movement. From January 2002 through October 2016, the correlation is only 0.31 (**Exhibit 3.5**).

EXHIBIT 3.5. CORRELATION OF MONTHLY RETURNS, JANUARY 2002–JUNE 2017

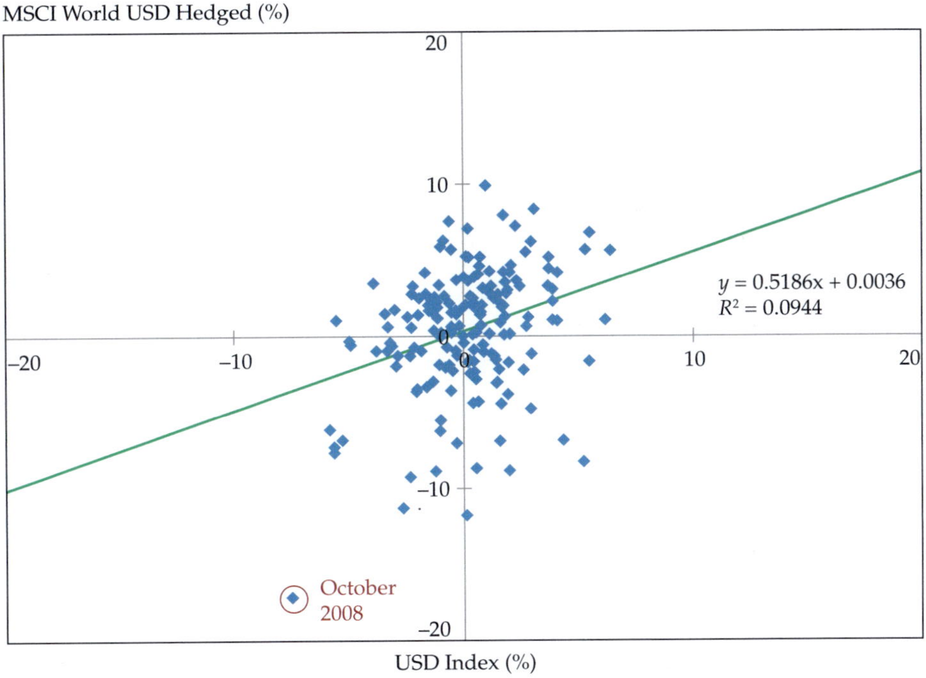

Source: William Blair.

[18]The USD Index is the US Dollar Index (DXY), which is based on the euro, yen, pound, Swedish krona, and Swiss franc.

As **Exhibit 3.6** illustrates, in instances where the hedged MSCI World declines more than 3% in a month, the correlation does not increase from 0.31; rather, it drops to 0.11, making it a better diversifier on relatively large market declines.

Lastly, as the lower-than-equity volatility dictates, the extremity of exchange rate misvaluations generally is less than those of equities.

This means that a meaningful allocation of risk capital to dynamic currency management can assist greatly in meeting DAA objectives.

In our investment taxonomy, DAA and GTAA are implementable in the traditional active, global macro, and active currency strategies.

EXHIBIT 3.6. CORRELATION OF MONTHLY RETURNS (MSCI DOWN > 3%), JANUARY 2002–JUNE 2017

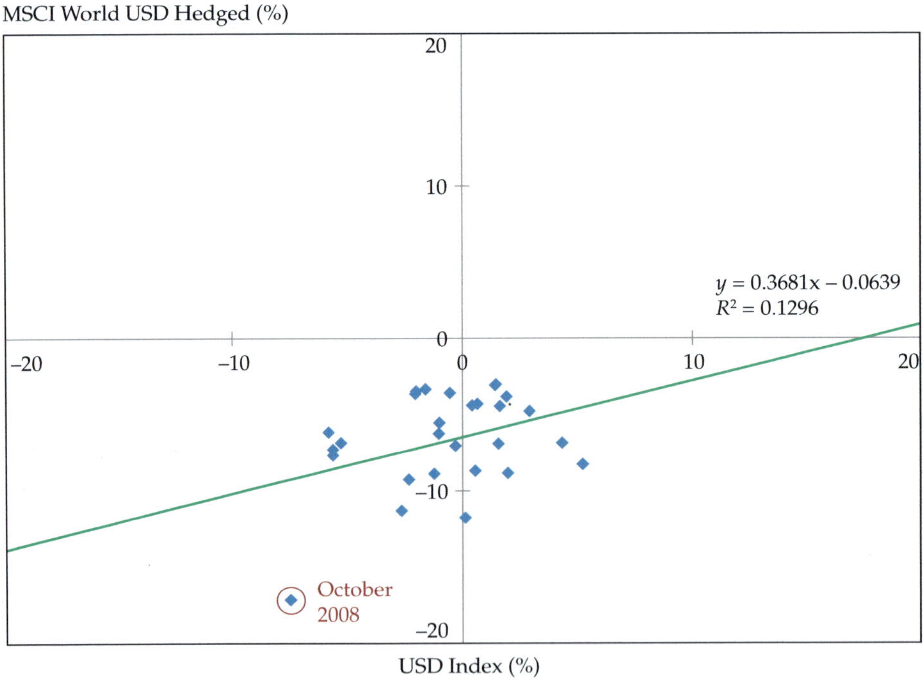

Source: William Blair.

These are denoted in Exhibit 3.2. If the intent is to "ride the tide" of intrinsic value over intermediate investment horizons, DAA is appropriate. However, if the intent is to "navigate the waves" of market behavior borne from geopolitical developments, central bank actions, and other one-off events, it is best to pursue a GTAA approach. DAA and GTAA are not mutually exclusive. Portfolios managed according to the intrinsic value discipline but with requisite shorter-term horizons should be composed of DAA for riding the tides and GTAA for navigating the waves.

3.5. RISK MANAGEMENT

Liquid alternative strategies afford more precise and different risk exposures than previously available. As a result, the primary risk contribution of these strategies is diversification. Although many of these strategies are hired for anticipated downside protection, there is no free lunch. Downside protection is insurance and comes at the cost of continual premium payment. For long put positions, the option premium paid is the cost of insurance. Generally, the cost would be the same for strategies that sell for protection as markets go down and buy for exposure as they rise. These are simply put option replication strategies and are expected to have exactly the same compensation as a long put position.

Downside limitation can come from higher expected returns for a specific risk level, reduced risk, or increased diversification. High-return expectations are not an expected risk, but if the returns are sufficiently high, the tail risk is not reduced but is shifted higher, becoming less or non-negative. Reduced risk is simply moving pro rata from the risky strategy into riskless assets—moving the risk down and the tail above a zero return. Despite some events that drive correlations higher, increased diversification remains a true investment free lunch. Diversification is not a panacea, but it helps reduce downside tail risk, or black swan, portfolio events.

Lastly, the "Holy Grail" of risk management is creating an anti-fragile portfolio. Unfortunately, building an anti-fragile portfolio is easier said than done. But advances are being derived from agent-based models and critical state theory. In particular, self-organized criticality, like the self-organized interactions in a market, is a state in which the next interaction would be expected to have an outcome magnitude that is inversely related to the outcome probability, such as a falling grain of sand sparking a likely jostling of an adjacent grain or an unlikely avalanche. In this state, the relationship is known but the probability is unknown. Self-organized criticality is simply an environment that is subject to a high-magnitude event.

3.6. CONCLUSION

Top-down investing is evolving rapidly. Sources of return enhancement that were previously the domain of active bottom-up and hedge fund portfolios are being exploited by liquid active and passive top-down managers. Active risk premiums, risk parity, and currency strategies are capturing these return sources by dynamically and tactically taking systematic risk exposures. Passive smart beta strategies specify rules for deviating from market-cap index weights to a different set of rules-based weights. The rules are specified to acquire and sustain risk exposures expected to be systematically compensated over time. A primary characterization of all active or passive top-down liquid alternative strategies is exposure to systematically compensated risks. Some have equities and bonds on individual companies, but the positions are driven by top-down considerations and are a minority of strategy risk exposures.

The categories of liquid alternative strategies should continue to increase in number as more exploitable systematic risks are identified and to capture more capital owing to their efficiency and low cost. As this trend continues, the industry will continue to evolve and new taxonomies will emerge.

4. RISK PARITY: SILVER BULLET OR A BRIDGE TOO FAR?

Gregory C. Allen

4.1. INTRODUCTION

Risk parity is a class of investment strategies in which capital is allocated across asset classes so that each asset class contributes an equal amount of volatility to the total volatility of the portfolio. Because this approach favors larger allocations to lower-returning asset classes, leverage is used to achieve the desired expected return. By contrast, the typical institutional investment portfolio uses an unlevered approach in which equities typically contribute roughly 90% of the total portfolio volatility. Advocates of risk parity argue that the traditional approach is unduly dependent on equities and is thus less efficient than a more risk-balanced approach. This argument proved compelling in the wake of the global financial crisis in 2008, allowing risk parity strategies to gain significant traction with institutional investors.

In this chapter, I evaluate the risk parity argument from a theoretical standpoint using the modern portfolio theory (MPT) framework of Markowitz (1952) and Tobin (1958). I then examine the historical performance (both simulated and actual) of risk parity portfolios relative to traditional portfolios used by institutional investors. Finally, I discuss the evolution of risk parity strategies and the prevalence of their use by institutional investors.

4.2. THE RISK PARITY PORTFOLIO AND MODERN PORTFOLIO THEORY

To better understand the theoretical basis of the risk parity portfolio, it is helpful to examine it in the context of the MPT framework. Specifically, by comparing a risk parity portfolio with traditional mean–variance-optimized portfolios along the efficient frontier, we can understand the differences in composition and the role that leverage plays in achieving the expected return.

Exhibit 4.1 shows the composition of a risk parity portfolio that includes US equity, non-US equity, real estate, commodities, and fixed income. The portfolio was developed using long-term assumptions for standard deviation and correlation, as shown in **Exhibit 4.2**. Unlike mean–variance optimization, there is little consensus among practitioners on the exact methodology for determining the risk parity portfolio. The most simplistic approach ignores correlations between asset classes, arguing that they are unstable and their use leads to increased estimation error. Under that approach, the asset class weights are determined by taking the inverse of their standard deviations and scaling them so that their sum equals 1. In this analysis, I use a methodology that allows both standard deviation and correlation estimates to determine the marginal contribution of each asset class to overall portfolio risk. This approach allows us to solve for the unique portfolio in which the marginal contributions of each asset class to total portfolio risk are equal. This methodology approximates the approach described in Qian (2006). In practice, this technique results in portfolios that better approximate the "optimal portfolio" on the efficient frontier in terms of both composition and risk level. Notably, neither of these approaches requires assumptions for expected return in order

EXHIBIT 4.1. RISK PARITY PORTFOLIO

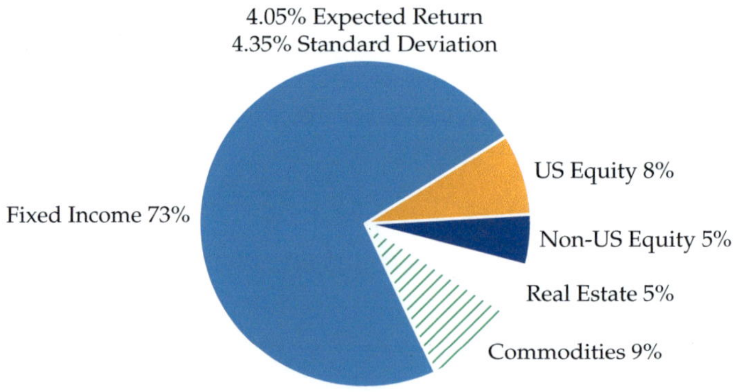

EXHIBIT 4.2. CAPITAL MARKET ASSUMPTIONS, RETURN, STANDARD DEVIATION, AND CORRELATION

Asset Class	US Equity	Non-US Equity	Real Estate	Commodities	Fixed Income
Expected Return	6.85	6.75	5.75	2.65	3.00
Standard Deviation	18.25	19.70	16.35	18.30	3.75

Expected Correlations

Asset Class	US Equity	Non-US Equity	Real Estate	Commodities	Fixed Income
US Equity	1.00				
Non-US Equity	0.84	1.00			
Real Estate	0.73	0.66	1.00		
Commodities	0.15	0.16	0.20	1.00	
Fixed Income	−0.11	−0.11	−0.03	−0.10	1.00

to determine the allocation between asset classes. Return expectations are required, however, to determine the appropriate amount of leverage to achieve a given level of expected return.

An efficient mean–variance portfolio with a 6.00% expected return is shown in **Exhibit 4.3** for comparison purposes. The efficient mean–variance portfolio was derived using the same set of assumptions for standard deviation and correlation that were used to derive the risk parity portfolio. It also uses assumptions for expected returns that are required by the mean–variance framework (shown in Exhibit 4.2). This portfolio was chosen because its risk posture is similar to that of the typical multi-asset-class portfolio used by institutional investors. In practice, the volatility of this portfolio is almost completely determined by the equity components, with fixed income contributing less than 5% to the total portfolio volatility.

Under the long-term assumptions shown in Exhibit 4.2, the unlevered risk parity portfolio has an expected return that is roughly 2% lower

EXHIBIT 4.3. MEAN-VARIANCE PORTFOLIO

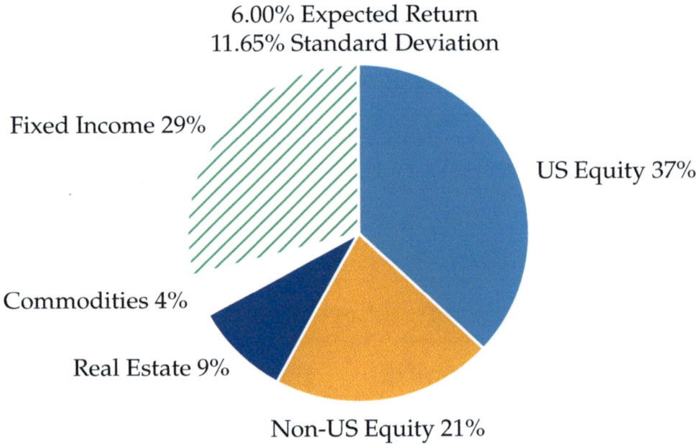

than that of the mean–variance portfolio (4.05% versus 6.00%). That is because over 70% of the risk parity portfolio is allocated to fixed income, which has an expected return of only 3%. The other higher-volatility asset classes have roughly equal weights in the portfolio. Notably, commodities have a meaningful allocation in the risk parity portfolio in spite of their low-return expectations. That is because return is ignored when solving for the risk parity portfolio, and the methodology in this example uses correlations. In the mean–variance portfolio, in which asset classes are penalized for having low expected returns, commodities receive a much smaller allocation.

The MPT framework helps explain how the use of leverage can bridge the 195 bp gap between the two portfolios. **Exhibit 4.4** depicts the efficient frontier generated using the long-term capital market assumptions in Exhibit 4.3. Each point along the efficient frontier represents the return-maximizing portfolio for that particular level of risk. These points collectively represent the efficient opportunity set for investors who do not use leverage. The 6.00% expected return portfolio from Exhibit 4.3 is shown for reference purposes.

Exhibit 4.5 adds the capital allocation line, which expands the framework to allow for the use of leverage (Tobin 1958). The intercept for the line is the borrowing rate (assumed to be 2.25% in this

EXHIBIT 4.4. EFFICIENT FRONTIER

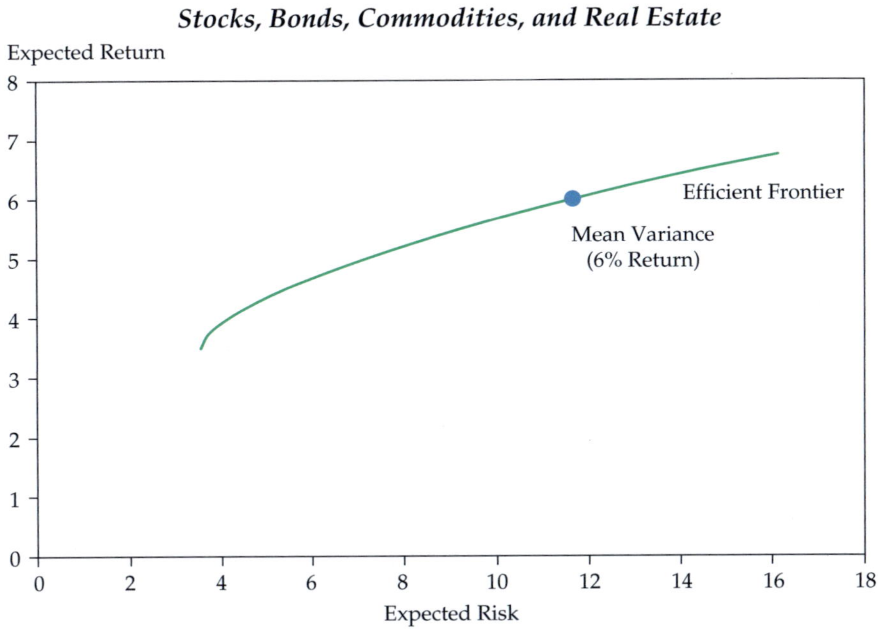

example). It is assumed that the investor can borrow or loan at this rate with no transaction costs. The slope of the capital allocation line is determined by finding its tangency point with the efficient frontier. The asset mix on the efficient frontier at the tangency point is considered the "optimal portfolio." The expected return and standard deviation for points on the capital allocation line to the left of the tangency point can be achieved by combining the optimal portfolio with cash. The expected return and risk for points on the capital allocation line to the right of the tangency point can be obtained by using leverage (borrowing money and investing it in the optimal portfolio).

In this example, the optimal portfolio has an expected return of roughly 4%. To achieve a return equal to that of the mean–variance portfolio, the optimal portfolio would need to be levered approximately 100%. Notably, the levered optimal portfolio has an expected standard

EXHIBIT 4.5. EFFICIENT FRONTIER AND CAPITAL ALLOCATION LINE

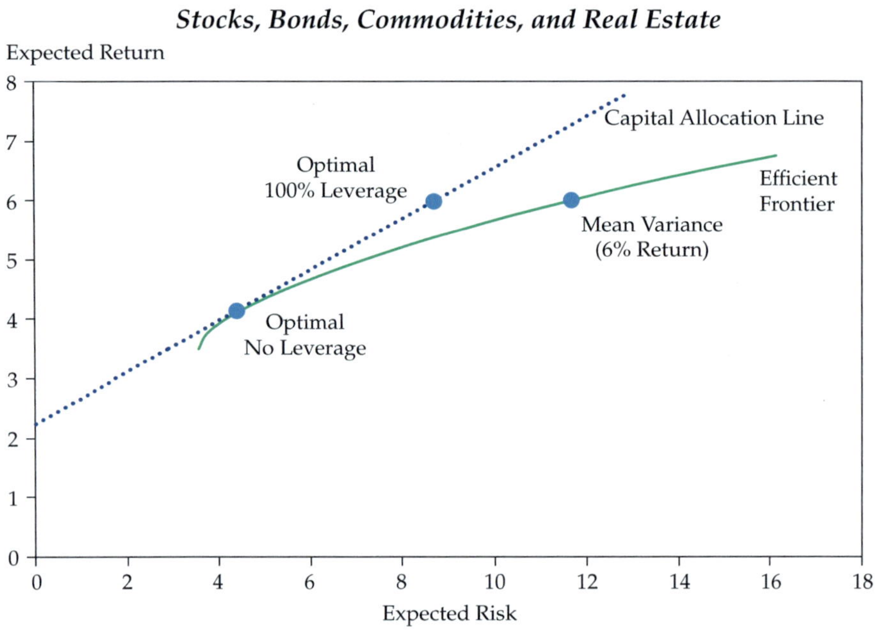

deviation approximately 25% lower than that of the mean–variance portfolio with the same expected return (an 8.70% standard deviation versus 11.65%). This example illustrates the promise of leverage, a key element of the risk parity approach.

Central to the risk parity value proposition is the question of how close the expected return and risk of the risk parity portfolio are to those of the optimal portfolio (i.e., do they reside on the efficient frontier in the same general area of risk?). **Exhibit 4.6** is designed to illustrate how important this is.

Exhibit 4.6 depicts the capital allocation line for a theoretical risk parity portfolio that resides below the efficient frontier (suboptimal). In this case, 100% leverage is needed simply to get back to the efficient frontier. An additional 30% leverage would be needed to achieve the targeted 6% expected return of the mean–variance portfolio. The resulting risk

EXHIBIT 4.6. EFFICIENT FRONTIER, CAPITAL ALLOCATION LINE, AND RISK PARITY PORTFOLIO

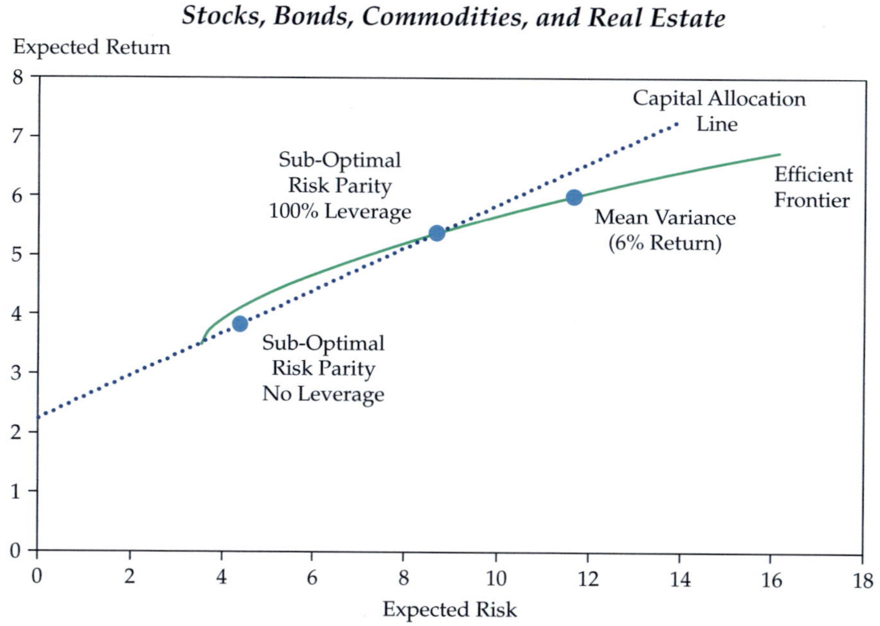

reduction of this 130% levered suboptimal risk parity portfolio relative to the 6% mean–variance portfolio is substantially diminished.

The MPT framework allows us to see that risk parity is an extension of the mean–variance approach with the added degree of freedom created through the explicit use of leverage. This insight leads to two important questions that are critical to evaluating the risk parity value proposition. The first is whether the risk parity portfolio lies on the efficient frontier—that is, does it deliver the maximum expected return on an unlevered basis for its expected level of risk? The second question is whether the capital allocation line is actually linear and sufficiently steep—that is, is the borrowing rate sufficiently low relative to the premium for risky assets to warrant the use of leverage, and is the cost of leverage constant relative to the amount of leverage used?

4.3. RISK PARITY AND EFFICIENCY

The question of whether the risk parity portfolio is efficient is important because this approach requires the use of leverage. As we saw in the previous section, leveraging an inefficient portfolio effectively flattens the slope of the capital allocation line, resulting in the need for greater leverage and diminishing the advantage of the levered portfolio relative to unlevered portfolios along the efficient frontier.

From the standpoint of theory, it would be pure coincidence if the risk parity portfolio and the optimal portfolio were exactly the same. That is because expected return is not used in the derivation of the risk parity portfolio, while it is a critical input in determining portfolios along the efficient frontier. This makes it extremely unlikely that the risk parity portfolio lies on the efficient frontier, let alone on the frontier *and* at the same spot as the optimal portfolio. Thus, we should accept the fact that in a purely theoretical sense, the levered risk parity portfolio is at best equal to (and probably inferior to) the levered optimal portfolio in terms of efficiency.

In practice, therefore, the question becomes, Is the risk parity portfolio a close enough approximation of the optimal portfolio to deliver on the promise of higher risk-adjusted returns? Asness, Frazzini, and Pedersen (2012) have argued that the two portfolios are sufficiently similar. They acknowledge that this is primarily because both portfolios overweight low-returning asset classes, rather than there being something special about all asset classes contributing equal risk. The advantage of overweighting lower-returning asset classes, they argue, is driven by a market inefficiency they call "leverage aversion," which they believe is sufficiently powerful to make up for any lack of efficiency on the part of the risk parity portfolio.

In simple terms, leverage aversion is the tendency of some investors to overweight risky assets relative to safer assets (presumably because they are either averse to leverage or cannot access it efficiently). This elevates the prices of risky assets relative to safer assets and results in safer assets having persistently higher risk-adjusted returns. A levered portfolio made up primarily of safer assets can take advantage of this inefficiency to generate superior risk-adjusted returns so long as it is reasonably close to the efficient frontier and leverage is sufficiently cheap.

Although empirical evidence seems to support the persistence of the leverage aversion effect (Asness, Frazzini, and Pedersen 2012; Frazzini and Pedersen 2014), that does not excuse practitioners from attempting to implement truly efficient risk parity portfolios. In practice, this often results in the relaxation of the "parity" constraint for such asset classes as commodities, which have inferior risk-adjusted returns relative to other risky assets (in many cases, they are simply excluded).

Some of the other key portfolio construction decisions that must be made in building efficient risk parity portfolios include the following: which asset classes to include; how many asset classes to include; defining the asset classes broadly or narrowly; the time horizon for measuring variance and covariance; how often the portfolio is rebalanced; how such illiquid assets as private equity and real estate should be included, and if they are included, how to measure their variance and covariance; and finally, how much leverage should be applied and how it should be structured.

It is beyond the scope of this chapter to address all these questions. For the most part, they are the same questions faced by managers of traditional unlevered institutional multi-asset class portfolios. In the next section, I will examine the one question on the list that is unique to the risk parity approach: the use of leverage.

4.4. RISK PARITY AND LEVERAGE

When James Tobin proposed the capital allocation line in 1958, there was a wide gap between the theory and the practical reality of leverage. In theory, you could borrow and loan virtually unlimited amounts of capital at the risk-free rate with no transaction costs. In practice, access to cost-effective leverage, particularly for the purpose of buying securities, was virtually nonexistent. Since that time, the capital markets have evolved considerably and institutional investors have access to a myriad of leverage sources—ranging from simple lines of credit, to the futures and options markets, to private party swaps, to CDOs and other exotic instruments with embedded leverage—all of which makes the prospect of implementing a risk parity portfolio much more tenable from a cost-efficiency standpoint. It also makes it substantially more complicated to identify and implement the optimal mix of leverage sources on an ongoing basis. Periods of market stress further complicate this problem.

In our simple example where we assumed that the borrowing rate was 2.25%, the risk parity portfolio required approximately 100% leverage to achieve the expected return of the 6% mean–variance portfolio. If we were to drop the borrowing rate from 2.25% to 1.75%, the amount of leverage required to achieve an expected return of 6% would decline to roughly 80% and the risk reduction relative to the mean–variance portfolio would improve accordingly, as illustrated in **Exhibit 4.7**.

This example highlights the fact that relatively minor changes in the borrowing rate can affect the required leverage ratio for a risk parity portfolio with a targeted level of return.

Changes that occur on the asset side of the equation can also influence the required leverage ratio. At the time that the assumptions for this example were developed, quantitative easing and other macro factors had driven the expected premium for risky assets to very low levels. Furthermore, low yields combined with a historically high representation of government-backed bonds had driven the expected volatility of the bond market down to historical lows. In a risk parity framework, a reduction in bond volatility necessitates more bonds in the portfolio to allow them to contribute their equal share of risk. The combination of a high representation of bonds in the portfolio and low expected returns on risky assets results in a historically low expected return for the unlevered risk parity portfolio. The lower the expected return relative to the borrowing rate (a flatter capital allocation line), the greater the amount of leverage needed to achieve the targeted return.

EXHIBIT 4.7. EFFICIENT FRONTIER, CAPITAL ALLOCATION LINE, AND MEAN-VARIANCE PORTFOLIO

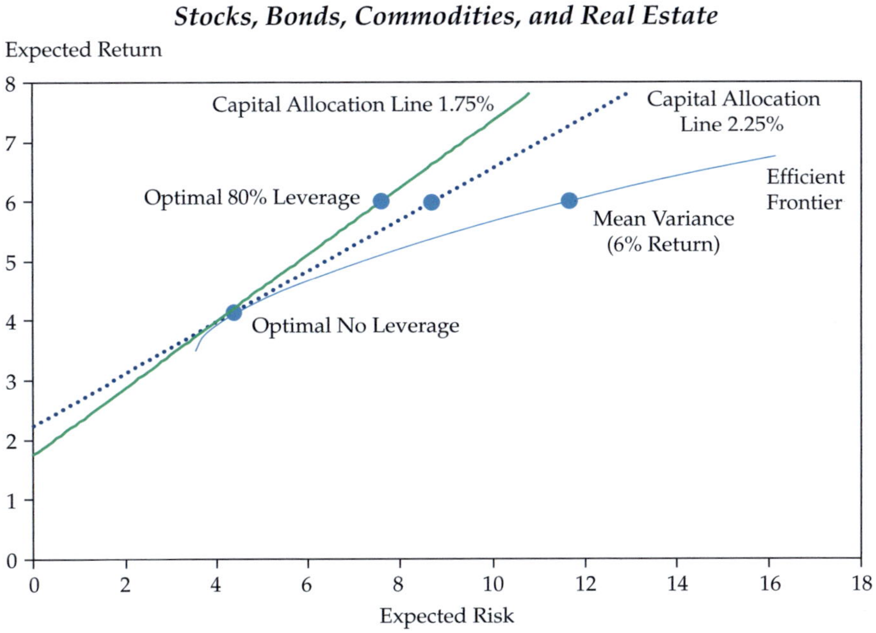

The fact that a flat capital allocation line results in an increase in required leverage raises the question of whether the cost of borrowing is constant relative to the amount of borrowing—that is, Is the capital allocation line actually linear, or does the slope flatten with the percentage of leverage used? In our example, the risk parity portfolio required 100% leverage to achieve the targeted level of return. It makes sense that as the amount of leverage on the portfolio increases, counterparties will demand greater compensation for the increased credit risk they bear. During periods of market dislocation when liquidity is at a premium, counterparties will demand an even higher premium or possibly withdraw their credit lines altogether for highly leveraged portfolios. A negatively sloped yield curve may also pose a challenge for maintaining the leverage required by the risk parity approach. When the short-term borrowing rate exceeds the yield on a market-oriented bond portfolio, it effectively results in a negatively sloped capital allocation line. Borrowing at the short-term rate and leveraging the portfolio under these circumstances will theoretically push it even further below the efficient frontier.

Finally, the introduction of systematic leverage will require advances in the monitoring, benchmarking, reporting, and risk-management tools used by institutional investors. Although banks and insurance companies have long used tools that look at both the debt side and the equity side of the portfolio to monitor risk and measure success or failure, the tools used by the typical pension fund or endowment focus almost exclusively on equity. Developing and implementing systems to capture data and analyze the complex interactions between a sophisticated multi-asset-class portfolio and the financing portfolio designed to support it will probably prove to be a challenge and a potential opportunity for custodians, consultants, and the investment staffs charged with the oversight of levered institutional portfolios.

4.5. RISK PARITY PERFORMANCE

Practitioners have provided substantial evidence, both through history and across global markets, that the risk parity approach would have historically delivered superior risk-adjusted returns relative to a traditional unlevered mean–variance portfolio. Asness et al. (2012) have undertaken perhaps the most careful and thorough analysis currently available in the literature. They simulated the performance of a risk parity portfolio relative to a 60/40 portfolio over 1926–2010 in the US market. They also analyzed 10 other developed markets globally over 1986–2010. In every case, the risk parity approach delivered higher risk-adjusted returns than the traditional 60/40 portfolio. In the case of the US portfolios, they tested five different borrowing rates, ranging from T-bills (the cheapest) to LIBOR (the most expensive). Their conclusions favoring the risk parity approach were robust across the entire set, although the advantage diminished meaningfully as the cost of leverage increased.

To provide further evidence, we can compare a risk parity portfolio to a mean–variance portfolio over the 20-year period ended

31 December 2016. Note that this was a particularly good time for risk parity, because the period was characterized by two major crises in the global equity markets: a consistently upwardly sloping yield curve and a general decline in interest rates. The exercise is still worthwhile, however, because it provides some color around the patterns of performance that yielded the superior risk-adjusted results. The two portfolios are constructed using the same set of asset classes detailed in the first section.[1] **Exhibit 4.8** reports the historical returns, standard deviations, and correlations for each asset class over the period.

Both portfolios are assumed to maintain a constant asset allocation over the period and are rebalanced quarterly. The risk parity portfolio is assumed to maintain a constant amount of leverage. The risk parity portfolio is derived using the approach discussed earlier that allows standard deviations and correlations to solve for the portfolio, whereby each asset class contributes the same marginal risk to the total. The borrowing rate is assumed to be equal to one-month LIBOR. The historical returns over the period are used to determine the constant leverage ratio of roughly 65%, which is needed to generate exactly a 7.5% annualized return. The mean–variance portfolio is derived using the same set of historical inputs. To make the comparison with the risk parity portfolio more intuitive, the portfolio along the efficient frontier that generated a 7.5% annualized return is chosen. The composition of the two portfolios is shown in **Exhibit 4.9**.

Neither portfolio closely resembles the portfolios used by large institutional investors over the last 20 years. The mean–variance portfolio benefits from knowing in advance the return patterns of each asset class and wisely assigns zero weights to both commodities

[1]The indexes used to represent each asset class are as follows:

1. US equity: Russell 3000 Index
2. Non-US equity: MSCI EAFE Index for Q1 1997 through Q4 2000 and MSCI ACWI ex-US Index for Q1 2001 through Q4 2016
3. Real estate: FTSE NAREIT Composite Index
4. Commodities: Goldman Sachs Commodities Index
5. Fixed income: Bloomberg Barclays Aggregate Index

EXHIBIT 4.8. RETURN, STANDARD DEVIATION, AND CORRELATION FOR 20 YEARS ENDED 31 DECEMBER 2016

Asset Class	US Equity	Non-US Equity	Real Estate	Commodities	Fixed Income
Return	7.86	4.35	9.02	−1.92	5.29
Standard Deviation	17.28	19.75	19.83	25.04	3.51

Expected Correlations

Asset Class	US Equity	Non-US Equity	Real Estate	Commodities	Fixed Income
US Equity	1.00				
Non-US Equity	0.88	1.00			
Real Estate	0.60	0.54	1.00		
Commodities	0.21	0.34	0.24	1.00	
Fixed Income	−0.35	−0.29	0.04	−0.18	1.00

and international equities. The risk parity portfolio includes everything it is offered regardless of return but perfectly balances the marginal contribution to risk across the asset classes over the 20-year period.

As expected, the risk parity portfolio generated the same return as the mean–variance portfolio with roughly 60% of the volatility over the period, resulting in a higher Sharpe ratio (0.90 versus 0.62) and substantially reduced drawdowns during the 2001–02 and 2008–09 crises relative to the mean–variance portfolio. **Exhibit 4.10** depicts the cumulative return of the risk parity portfolio relative to the mean–variance portfolio over the period. It allows us to see exactly which periods risk parity had an advantage and which ones it did not.

The shaded areas indicate the periods when the risk parity portfolio would have outperformed the mean–variance portfolio. With its reduced exposure to equity risk and increased exposure to interest rate risk, the risk parity portfolio would have weathered the bursting of the

EXHIBIT 4.9. COMPOSITION OF MEAN–VARIANCE PORTFOLIO AND RISK PARITY PORTFOLIO LEVERAGED 65%

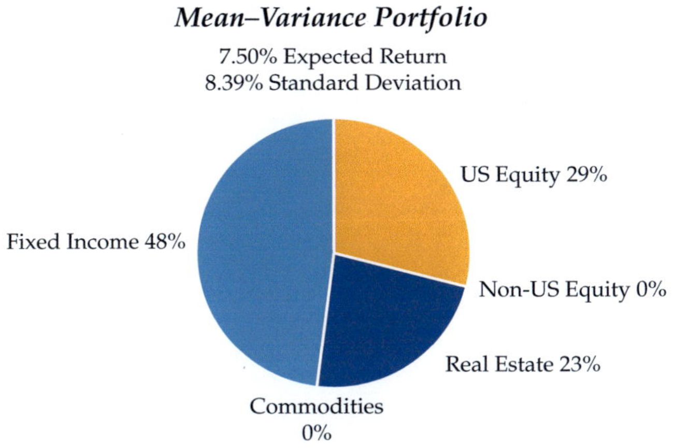

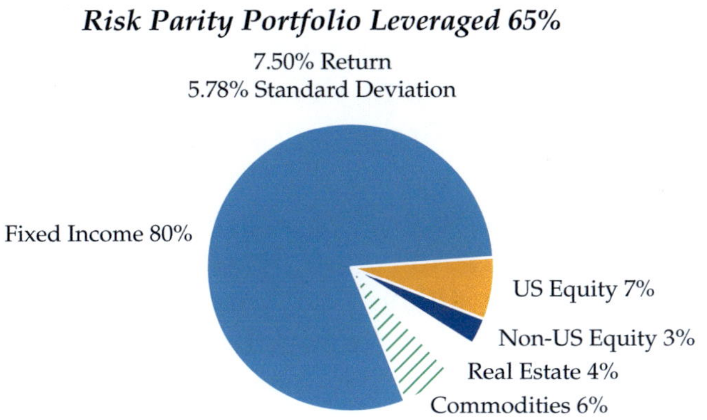

dot-com bubble and the global financial crisis better than the mean–variance portfolio. During periods of strong equity performance, however, the risk parity approach would have consistently trailed.

Exhibit 4.11 illustrates the repercussions of this performance pattern in the context of the Callan Total Fund Sponsor Database, a broad universe of over 1,500 public and corporate pension funds, foundations, endowments, and other pools of institutional capital.

EXHIBIT 4.10. CUMULATIVE RETURN RELATIVE TO MEAN–VARIANCE PORTFOLIO FOR 20 YEARS ENDED 31 DECEMBER 2016

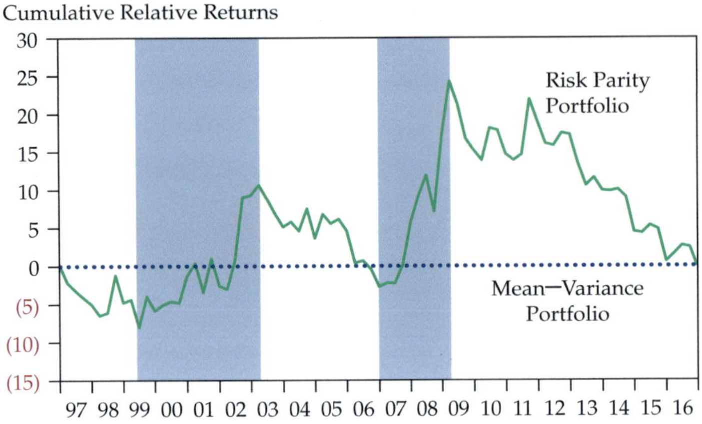

As Exhibit 4.11 shows, the performance ranking of the risk parity portfolio would have been quite volatile over the period, bouncing around from the bottom to the top of this broad distribution of diversified multi-asset-class portfolios. This pattern indicates that although a risk parity strategy might have been a good diversifier as a component of one of these portfolios, it would have been very difficult to maintain the risk parity approach at the policy level for a large institutional investor. Very few, if any, institutions have the patience and perspective to stick with a program that has the potential to land them in the 99th percentile relative to peers over a five-year period. This helps explain the fact that although there has been almost no adoption of the risk parity approach at the policy level among institutional investors, many of them have carved out strategic allocations to the approach as part of their overall asset allocation.

4.6. US INSTITUTIONAL HISTORY OF RISK PARITY

Although the risk parity approach has been pitched as a superior alternative to the traditional unlevered mean–variance-efficient portfolios favored by institutions, there has been only one case of a large public institution attempting to adopt it at the policy level. Coming out of

EXHIBIT 4.11. RETURN RANKINGS FOR FIVE-YEAR PERIODS

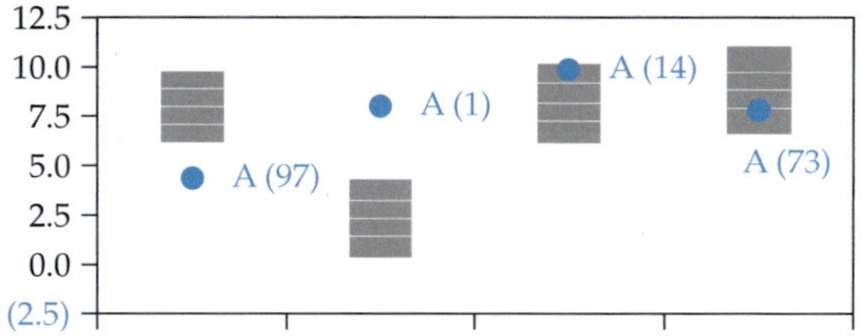

	12/31/16	12/31/11	12/31/06	12/31/01
10th Percentile	9.79	4.31	10.17	11.06
25th Percentile	9.08	3.17	9.31	9.90
Median	8.17	2.18	8.31	8.76
75th Percentile	7.19	1.24	7.24	7.69
90th Percentile	6.18	0.37	6.14	6.60
Risk Parity Portfolio ● A	4.38	8.01	9.88	7.82

Source: Callan.

the global financial crisis in 2009, the San Diego County Employees Retirement Association (SDCERA) was looking for an alternative to the standard equity-centric approach that had allowed it to lose over $2 billion (peak to trough) during the crisis. The SDCERA ultimately outsourced the management of the entire portfolio to Integrity Capital (since merged with Salient Partners), which implemented a risk parity strategy at the total portfolio level. The experiment was abandoned in July 2015, after the SDCERA portfolio had consistently trailed peers during the seven-year bull market for equities that followed the crisis (McDonald 2015). This episode highlights the challenge for institutions of pursuing an investment policy that is fundamentally different from the approach used by peers. By all accounts, the SDCERA portfolio was delivering on its promise of lower volatility, but in a bull equity market, this took the form of lower returns relative to peers. Sadly, the strategy was abandoned before the flip side of the volatility reduction equation could be fully realized.

Given the difficulty of pursuing risk parity at the policy level, the preponderance of institutional adoption has been in the form of incremental allocations to the strategy, either as part of an "absolute return" allocation or as a fully dedicated risk parity allocation. Generally, these allocations have been in the range of 3%–5% of the portfolio and have been implemented by investing with managers who specialize in the approach. There is some debate regarding which firm first offered a risk parity product, but a good argument can be made that Ray Dalio and Bob Prince of Bridgewater Associates were the first to implement it at an institutional level with their "All Weather" portfolio, launched in 1996. It was not until 2005, however, that the term *risk parity* was coined in a white paper written by Edward Qian (2005) of PanAgora Asset Management. In the years since the 2008 financial crisis, roughly two dozen firms have launched products in the United States designed and marketed around the concept of risk parity; as of 31 December 2016, total assets managed across these strategies exceeded $120 billion.[2] **Exhibit 4.12** provides a list of the firms that had submitted data on risk parity strategies to either the Callan Global Manager Research Database or the eVestment Global Database as of that date.

As risk parity passes through its first decade since the term was coined (and its second decade since the launch of the original "All Weather" strategy), the products being marketed under the moniker continue to evolve. Many practitioners have adopted an explicitly tactical (or dynamic) approach to implementing risk parity, constantly shifting their allocations across asset classes as well as their use of leverage to respond to changes in their outlook for expected returns and risks. Other practitioners have gone beyond the use of simple asset classes in their portfolio construction and have started to use "risk premiums" as the building blocks for their risk parity portfolios. A third category of managers has abandoned the strict interpretation of "parity" altogether in their risk allocations, focusing instead on optimizing risk-adjusted returns across their multi-asset-class portfolios. Complicating things even further is the fact that many of these strategies are offered at varying levels of targeted volatility to appeal to a broader array of investors. The end result is a universe of products that arguably have more differences than similarities. This can be seen in **Exhibit 4.13**, which contrasts the range of returns

[2]Callan Global Manager Research Database.

EXHIBIT 4.12. FIRMS WITH RISK PARITY PRODUCTS AS OF 31 DECEMBER 2016

AllianceBernstein, LP (AB)	JP Morgan Asset Management
Aquila Capital Investment	Neuberger Berman Group, LLC
AQR Capital Management	PanAgora Asset Management
BlackRock, Inc.	Parametric Portfolio Associates
Boston Advisors LLC	Pear Tree Funds
Bridgewater Associates, LP	Putnam Investments
Columbia Threadneedle Investments	Salient Partners, LP
First Quadrant, LP	Schroder Investment Management Limited
Fulcrum Asset Management	Wellington Management Company, LLP
Global Asset Management (GAM)	Zadia Gestion
Invesco, Ltd	
Janus Capital Group	

Sources: Callan Global Manager Research Database and eVestment Global Database.

across risk parity products with the range of returns across Callan's Total Fund Sponsor Database over the three-year period ended 31 December 2016.

As Exhibit 4.13 shows, the dispersion of returns across the risk parity universe over this fairly short period was significantly wider than that of the fund sponsor universe. The median return was also 211 bps lower, indicating that the typical experience with risk parity over the period had the effect of reducing the overall portfolio return. Exhibit 4.13 points out the importance when selecting a risk parity strategy of having a very clear understanding of how it is constructed, what its targeted risk level is over time, and how it can be expected to perform in a variety of market conditions.

4.7. CONCLUSION

After the global financial crisis, it is not surprising that institutional investors took an acute interest in alternatives to equitycentric

EXHIBIT 4.13 RETURNS FOR THREE YEARS ENDED 31 DECEMBER 2016 (RISK PARITY UNIVERSE VS. CALLAN TOTAL FUND SPONSOR UNIVERSE)

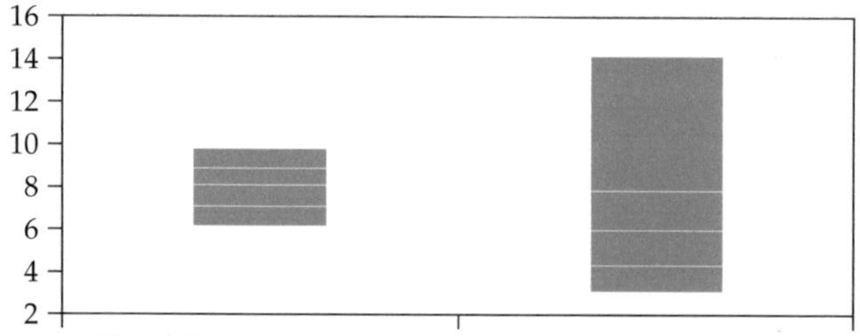

	Fund Sponsor Universe	Risk Parity Universe
10th Percentile	9.79	14.14
25th Percentile	9.08	7.84
Median	8.17	6.06
75th Percentile	7.19	4.36
90th Percentile	6.18	3.12

strategies. The fact that the previous 15 years had been characterized by two major crises in the global equity markets, a consistently upwardly sloping yield curve, and a general decline in interest rates made risk parity look like a particularly compelling option. Although concerns about peer risk and the use of leverage made adoption at the policy level untenable, many institutions carved out strategic allocations to risk parity in an effort to further diversify their portfolios. Practitioners have responded with a wide variety of products, and assets managed across these strategies have steadily grown. Questions remain about the use of leverage—specifically, levering fixed income—during a period of rising rates or one characterized by a persistently inverted yield curve. Practitioners argue, however, that interest rate risk is but one of many exposures in a well-balanced risk parity portfolio and that the approach will ultimately show its worth over the long run by delivering on its promise of a higher risk-adjusted return.

REFERENCES

Asness, Clifford S., Andrea Frazzini, and Lasse H. Pedersen. 2012. "Leverage Aversion and Risk Parity." *Financial Analysts Journal*, vol. 68, no. 1 (January/February): 47–59.

Boido, Claudio, and Giovanni Fulci. 2010. "A Risk Contribution Approach to Asset Allocation." *IUP Journal of Financial Risk Management*, vol. 7, no. 1–2: 58–77.

Frazzini, Andrea, and Lasse Heje Pedersen. 2014. "Betting against Beta." *Journal of Financial Economics*, vol. 111, no. 1 (January): 1–25.

Markowitz, Harry M. 1952. "Portfolio Selection." *Journal of Finance*, vol. 7, no. 1 (March): 77–91.

McDonald, Jeff. 2015. "Pension Fund Dismisses Texas Consultant." *San Diego Union Tribune* (16 July).

Qian, Edward. 2005. "Risk Parity Portfolios: Efficient Portfolios through True Diversification." White paper, PanAgora Asset Management (September).

———. 2006. "On the Financial Interpretation of Risk Contribution: Risk Budgets Do Add Up." *Journal of Investment Management*, vol. 4, no. 4: 41–51.

Tobin, James. 1958. "Liquidity Preference as Behavior towards Risk." *Review of Economic Studies*, vol. 25, no. 2 (February): 65–86.

5. THE MORNINGSTAR STYLE BOX

Jeffrey Ptak, CFA

5.1. EQUITY STYLE ANALYSIS: AN OVERVIEW

Equity style analysis is a method used to identify and describe the characteristics of an investment portfolio. Style analysis might reveal that one portfolio invests in large-cap, value-oriented securities whereas another invests in small-cap growth stocks. Individual investors use style to understand what types of investments they are buying and how they fit into existing portfolios. Financial advisers, money managers, and academics, among others, use style analysis to purchase, classify, or construct managed investments and to monitor them for style drift. Style analysis is also used to construct peer groups and to select appropriate style-specific benchmarks.

Although style analysis is widely regarded as a valuable exercise, there is much debate about how style should be measured. There are two main approaches to style analysis: holdings based and returns based. Holdings-based style tools classify portfolios on the basis of the characteristics of the underlying securities. For example, the Morningstar® Style Box™ is a holdings-based analysis of the size and value/growth orientation of the underlying stocks in a fund. In contrast, returns-based style analysis compares the portfolio's total returns (usually three to five years of monthly returns) with the total returns of various style-based indexes (usually 4 to 12 indexes) and makes inferences about style on the basis of how closely the portfolio returns resemble those of different indexes.

Returns-based style analysis has been more widely used among financial professionals, because the input data (monthly returns) are readily available. The alternative holdings-based approach has been well received in concept and enjoys increasingly widespread adoption in practice.

Morningstar has long been a proponent of holdings-based style analysis but recognizes that there may be situations where returns-based style analysis can also be helpful. Because the two approaches are so different, it is important to understand how the models work in order to correctly interpret the results. (For further details, see the "Appendix" section.)

5.2. HISTORY OF THE MORNINGSTAR STYLE BOX

The Morningstar Style Box was introduced in 1992 to help investors and advisers determine the investment style of a fund. Because different investment styles can exhibit varying levels of risk and returns, it is crucial that investors understand style and have a tool to measure their style exposure. In that way, the Morningstar Style Box offered an intuitive visual representation of style to help investors build more-cohesive portfolios that they could monitor more precisely.

In 1992, when the Style Box was launched, much of what passed for fund research simply projected past performance into the future. The Style Box sought to advance analysis by giving investors a way to layer evidence about the characteristics of a fund's equity holdings with other supporting data, such as historical returns. In so doing, investors could better assess the range of future possibilities and thus better diversify a portfolio of funds or establish peer groups by which to compare similar funds and evaluate performance.

The Style Box also offered investors a means to identify and monitor a fund's investment characteristics over time and ensure that it was being invested in a manner consistent with the fund's stated investment objective. Although not intended to be an all-encompassing measure of risk, the Style Box strove to detail basic characteristics of a fund's equity holdings in order to delineate risk–return trade-offs and the range of potential future outcomes. The interplay of multiple styles held meaning, and the Style Box sought to convey that meaning in an informative way.

Finally, the Style Box aimed to empower investors by taking the categorization choices out of fund marketers' hands (through their sometimes misleading or opaque naming conventions) and putting it in the hands of investors and their advocates. This proved to be a turning point in the way funds were presented and sold to investors, who now had a means of independently assessing what a fund did and making like-to-like comparisons with other funds in evaluating its merits.

5.3. OVERVIEW

Morningstar classifies funds as large-cap, mid-cap, or small-cap on the basis of the market capitalization of the fund's stock holdings and as value, blend, or growth on the basis of the value/growth orientation of the stock holdings. The nine possible combinations of these characteristics correspond to the nine squares of the Morningstar Style Box, as shown in **Exhibit 5.1**—size is displayed along the vertical axis and style is displayed along the horizontal axis.

The current Style Box model uses 10 factors—5 for value and 5 for growth—to measure a stock's value/growth orientation. The multifactor approach produces more accurate and stable stock and fund style assignments. To measure size, the enhanced model uses flexible rather than static breakpoints between large-, mid-, and small-cap stocks. The current methodology also measures stocks in the context of a geographic style zone, rather than grouping all non-US stocks together.

The methodology starts at the stock level and thus fosters a shared analytical framework that can also be applied to fund research, portfolio assembly, and market monitoring. In the United States, Morningstar introduced the enhanced 10-factor model for US stocks and US equity funds in May 2002 and for non-US stocks and global funds in March 2004. Outside the United States, the 10-factor model was introduced in various markets starting in March 2004. Morningstar applies the same methodology to all types of managed equity products, such as open-end mutual funds, closed-end funds, separate accounts, and so on.

EXHIBIT 5.1. THE MORNINGSTAR STYLE BOX

The Morningstar Style Box is a nine-square grid that illustrates the "investment style" of stocks and mutual funds. It classifies securities based on their market capitalization (the vertical axis) and growth and value factors (the horizontal axis).

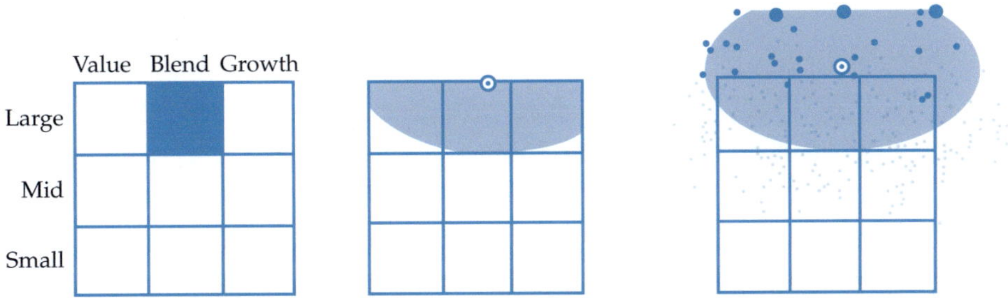

5.4. DRIVING PRINCIPLES

The following principles animate the Morningstar Style Box methodology and how it is meant to be applied in practice.

1. *The Style Box is applicable in all equity markets.* A geographic framework ensures that stocks are compared with their closest peers and that style assignments are relevant to local investors everywhere. World equity markets are divided into seven style zones: United States, Latin America, Canada, Europe, Japan, Asia ex-Japan, and Australia/New Zealand.
2. *Stock size breakpoints should be flexible and responsive to changing market conditions.* Instead of using fixed dollar breakpoints to classify securities as large-cap, mid-cap, or small-cap, the model bases that distinction on each stock's position in the cumulative capitalization of its style zone. Large-cap stocks are those that together account for the top 70% of the capitalization of each style zone, mid-cap stocks represent the next 20%, and small-caps represent the balance.
3. *A stock's value/growth orientation should be relative to a peer group.* A Japanese small-cap stock performs quite differently from a European large-cap stock, and the two should not be scored relative to each other. Therefore, two stocks may have similar financial

ratios and growth prospects, but they may be given different value/growth assignments if they are in different scoring groups.

4. *A stock's value orientation and growth orientation are distinct measures.* Thus, they are estimated using related but separate variables. Once estimated (Overall Value and Overall Growth scores), they are combined into a single net value-core-growth (VCG) score.
   - A high Overall Value score indicates that a stock's price is relatively low, given the anticipated per-share earnings, book value, revenues, cash flow, and dividends that the stock provides to investors. A high price relative to these measures indicates that a stock's value orientation is weak, but it does not necessarily mean that the stock is growth oriented.
   - A high Overall Growth score indicates that a stock's per share earnings, book value, revenues, and cash flow are expected to grow quickly relative to other stocks in the same scoring group. A weak growth orientation does not necessarily mean that a stock has a strong value orientation.
   - It follows that an individual stock may have any combination of strong or weak growth and value characteristics. Where one set of characteristics is dominant, the stock can be classified accordingly. Where the stock's growth and value characteristics are similar in strength, the stock will be given a "core" style assignment. (A note on terminology: For stocks, the central column of the Style Box represents the "core" style. For funds, both value and growth managers often hold core stocks for diversification or other reasons; therefore, the central column of the Style Box for funds represents the "blend" style.)

5. *Historical measures alone can rarely fully capture a stock's value/growth orientation.* Investors and institutions trade on the basis of historical measures as well as future expectations. Therefore, Morningstar includes both historical and forward-looking financial measures in the model to ensure that all information available to active fund managers is considered. The forward-looking measures are primarily based on third-party analysts' earnings estimates.

When available, forward-looking data contribute to 50% of the stock's style assignment.

6. *A stock's size and style orientation can be used for fund research, portfolio assembly, and monitoring.* Morningstar assigns *x*- and *y*-coordinates for style and size that form the building blocks for this unified framework for holdings-based analysis. This integrated system can help investors and advisers understand the style positioning of funds and construct well-diversified portfolios that are consistent with investors' return expectations and risk tolerances. Also, in the United States, investors can monitor the performance of their US portfolios with Morningstar's style-based market indexes, which offer broad coverage of the US market and are based on the same structural foundation as the Style Box.

To be sure, some have argued that the Style Box can limit fund managers by inculcating expectations that they will not stray from their assigned region of the Style Box. But the Style Box was never intended to drive conformity in the way fund managers invest or to dictate a fund's investing style. Rather, the Style Box seeks to describe and usefully depict a fund's risk tendencies and provide a framework investors can use to better assess the range of future outcomes, compare funds, and build portfolios. Like any tool, the Style Box can be misapplied in practice, leading to circumstances in which fund managers might feel impeded. But in practice, funds follow a wide range of approaches, reflected in the diversity of investment options available to investors.

Given this diversity, some have also asked whether the Style Box is capable of accurately depicting the full range of investment styles that managers ply. For instance, an all-cap or go-anywhere value investor might quarrel with the idea of being assigned to a *single* region of the Style Box. However, data suggest that the Style Box succeeds in grouping similar funds to facilitate comparison, differences notwithstanding. For instance, **Exhibit 5.2** tallies US equity funds on the basis of their correlation to the average fund in the Morningstar category to which they have been assigned (which, in turn, is a function of their Style Box classification).

EXHIBIT 5.2. DISTRIBUTION OF US EQUITY FUNDS BY CORRELATION OF RETURNS TO AVERAGE FUND IN ASSIGNED CATEGORY (THREE YEARS ENDED 12/31/16)

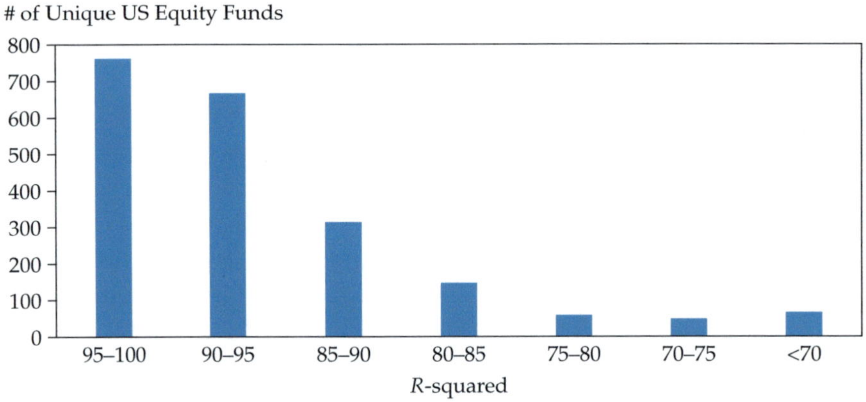

In situations where funds migrate from one style to another or do not fit tidily within a single style, the Style Box can still be leveraged to capture and relay this information in useful ways. For example, as further discussed later in this chapter, the "Morningstar Style Trail" tool builds on a fund's historical Style Box classifications to show investors where it has traveled in the Style Box over time. Investors seeking a more granular, refined view of a fund's style exposures can use the "Morningstar Ownership Zone," which complements the Style Box to provide an additional layer of detail about an equity portfolio's investment style. The Ownership Zone plots each stock in the portfolio within the Style Box and then shades the area that represents 75% of the assets in the portfolio while indicating the level of holdings concentration. The Ownership Zone is also addressed later in this chapter.

5.5. HOW THE STYLE BOX WORKS

The equity Style Box is a nine-square grid that classifies securities by size along the vertical axis and by value and growth characteristics along the horizontal axis. The Style Box, as shown in **Exhibit 5.3,** captures three of the major considerations in equity investing: size,

EXHIBIT 5.3. THE MORNINGSTAR STYLE BOX

Fund Investment Style

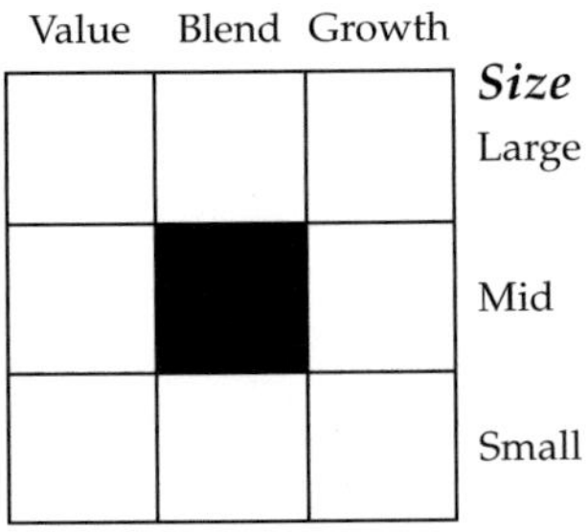

The Morningstar Style Box™ is a nine-square grid that illustrates the investment style of a security. Size (large, mid, or small) is displayed along the vertical axis, and style is displayed along the horizontal axis. The "value" and "growth" investment styles are common to both stocks and funds. For stocks, the central column of the Style Box represents the "core" style. Few or no funds contain only stocks with extreme value–growth orientations, and both value and growth managers often hold core stocks for diversification or other reasons. Therefore, for funds, the central column represents the "blend" style (a mixture of growth and value stocks or mostly core stocks).

security valuation, and security growth. Value and growth are measured separately because they are distinct concepts.

A stock's value orientation reflects the prices that investors are willing to pay for some combination of the stock's anticipated per-share earnings, book value, revenues, cash flow, and dividends. A high price relative to these measures indicates that a stock's value orientation is weak, but it does not necessarily mean that the stock is growth oriented. A stock's growth orientation is independent of its price and reflects the growth rate of such fundamental variables as earnings, book value, revenues, and cash flow. When neither value nor growth is dominant, stocks are classified as "core" and portfolios are classified as "blend."

In general, a growth-oriented portfolio will hold the stocks of companies that the manager believes will increase such factors as sales and earnings faster than the rest of the market. A value-oriented portfolio contains mostly stocks the manager thinks are currently undervalued in price and will eventually see their worth recognized by the market. A blend portfolio might be a mix of growth stocks and value stocks, or it might contain stocks that exhibit both characteristics.

Morningstar's equity style methodology uses a "building block," holdings-based approach that is consistent with Morningstar's fundamental approach to investing. Style is first determined at the stock level and then those attributes are "rolled up" to determine the overall investment style of a fund or portfolio. This unified framework can link what are often treated as separate processes—stock research, fund research, portfolio assembly, and market monitoring—in the belief that a shared analytical framework will lead to better portfolio construction and fund usage.

The vertical axis of the Style Box defines three size categories, or capitalization bands—small, midsize, and large. The horizontal axis defines three style categories. Two of these categories, value and growth, are common to both stocks and funds. However, for stocks, the central column of the style box represents the core style (those stocks in which neither value nor growth characteristics dominate); for funds, it represents the blend style (a mix of growth and value stocks or mostly core stocks).

Style Box assignments begin at the individual stock level. Morningstar determines the investment style of each individual stock in its database. Stocks are evaluated against other stocks in the same geographic area (United States, Latin America, Canada, Europe, Japan, Asia ex-Japan, Australia/New Zealand). The style attributes of individual stocks are then used to determine the style classification of stock mutual funds.

THE HORIZONTAL AXIS

The scores for a stock's value and growth characteristics determine its horizontal placement:

- Value score components and weights
  - Forward-looking measures, 50.0%
    - Price/prospective earnings
  - Historically based measures, 50.0%
    - Price/book, 12.5%
    - Price/sales, 12.5%

        - Price/cash flow, 12.5%
        - Dividend yield, 12.5%

- Growth score components and weights
    - Forward-looking measures, 50.0%
        - Long-term projected earnings growth
    - Historically based measures, 50.0%
        - Historical earnings growth, 12.5%
        - Sales growth, 12.5%
        - Cash flow growth, 12.5%
        - Book value growth, 12.5%

Growth and value characteristics for each individual stock are compared with those of other stocks within the same capitalization band and are scored from 0 to 100 for both value and growth. To determine the overall style score, the value score is subtracted from the growth score (**Exhibit 5.4**).

EXHIBIT 5.4. DETERMINING THE STYLE SCORE

Growth Score	0 to 100
⊖ Value Score	0 to 100
⊜ Style Score	–100 to 100

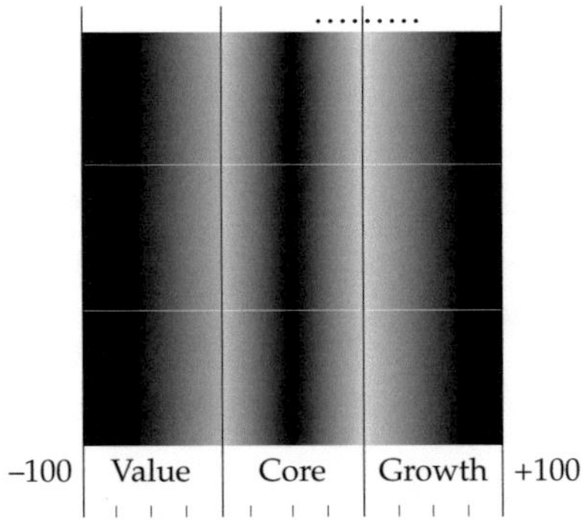

The resulting number can range from 100 (for low-yield, extremely growth-oriented stocks) to –100 (high-yield, low-growth stocks). A stock is classified as growth if the net score equals or exceeds the "growth threshold" (normally about 25 for large-cap stocks). It is deemed value if its score equals or falls below the "value threshold" (normally about –15 for large-cap stocks). If the score lies between the two thresholds, the stock is classified as core.

The thresholds between value, core, and growth stocks vary to some degree over time, as the distribution of stock styles changes in the market. However, on average, the three stock styles each account for approximately one-third of the total free float in each size category.

THE VERTICAL AXIS

Rather than a fixed number of "large-cap" or "small-cap" stocks, Morningstar uses a flexible system that is not adversely affected by overall movements in the market. Large-cap stocks are defined as the group that accounts for the top 70% of the capitalization of each geographic area, mid-cap stocks compose the next 20%, and small-cap stocks represent the balance.

MOVING FROM INDIVIDUAL STOCKS TO FUNDS

A stock fund is an aggregation of individual stocks, and its style is determined by the style assignments of the stocks it owns. By plotting all of a fund's stocks on the stock style grid, the range of stock styles in the fund immediately becomes apparent. An asset-weighted average of the underlying stocks' style and size scores determines a fund's placement in the Style Box.

Style Box assignments for stocks are updated each month. Assignments for funds are recalculated whenever Morningstar receives updated portfolio holdings for the fund.

The Morningstar Style Box is applicable in all equity markets. A geographic framework ensures that style assignments are relevant to local investors everywhere. World equity markets are divided into seven style zones:

- United States
- Latin America
- Canada
- Europe
- Japan
- Asia ex-Japan
- Australia/New Zealand

The stocks in each style zone are further divided into large-, mid-, and small-cap groups for value/growth scoring. Style Box assignments for funds are based on the asset-weighted average of the style and size scores of the underlying stocks.

METHODOLOGICAL HISTORY

Morningstar's original Style Box model for equity funds used the median market capitalization of the underlying stocks to determine a fund's average size. The original model measured value/growth orientation on the basis of two price ratios (price-to-earnings and price-to-book ratios for US equity funds and price-to-book and price-to-cash-flow ratios for non-US equity funds). In the original model, all non-US stocks and funds were measured against a single set of breakpoints. In 2002, Morningstar revised the methodology to adopt the principles described earlier.

5.6. USING THE STYLE BOX

The Morningstar Style Box enjoys widespread use among individual investors, financial advisers, and institutions, who use it to compare, select, and monitor funds and build portfolios. What follows are some of the more common ways the Style Box has been applied in practice or leveraged within other analytics or tools that Morningstar offers.

MORNINGSTAR OWNERSHIP ZONE

Understanding how different types of stocks behave is crucial for building a diversified, style-controlled portfolio of stocks or mutual funds. The Morningstar Style Box helps investors construct portfolios on the basis of the characteristics—the style factors—of all the stocks and funds the portfolio contains.

The style and size scores for stocks and funds are the building blocks for the Morningstar Ownership Zone. A portfolio's Ownership Zone is derived by plotting each stock in the fund's portfolio within the proprietary Morningstar Style Box. The shaded area represents the central 75% of the fund's assets, providing an intuitive visual representation of the area of the market in which the fund invests. A "centroid" plot in the middle of the Ownership Zone represents the weighted average of all the fund's holdings.

The Ownership Zone can be illustrated on the familiar nine-square grid of the Morningstar Style Box (**Exhibit 5.5**).

The Style Box can be expanded to a 25-square grid. This version of the Ownership Zone often includes individual plot points for each stock (**Exhibit 5.6**), providing investors with more detail and allowing them to better differentiate between giant-cap, micro-cap, deep-value, and high-growth stocks.

EXHIBIT 5.5. THE OWNERSHIP ZONE (NINE-SQUARE GRID)

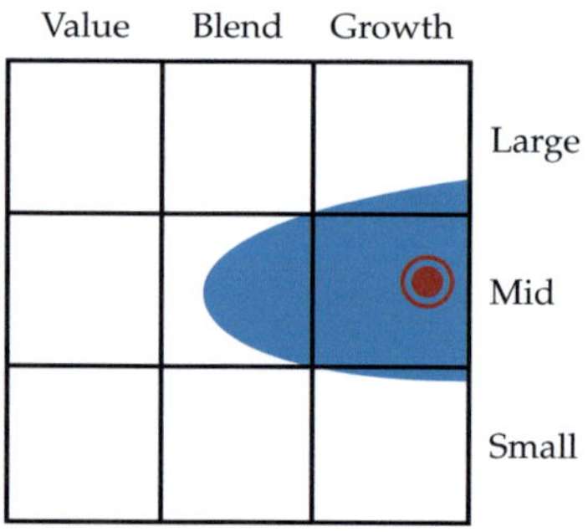

EXHIBIT 5.6. THE OWNERSHIP ZONE (25-SQUARE GRID)

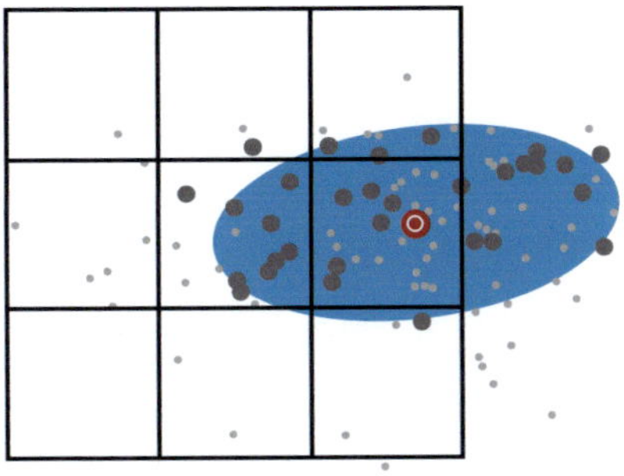

The Ownership Zone helps investors visually evaluate the investment style of a fund or portfolio. It can also help investors monitor style drift, a fund's tendency to change its style over time.

MORNINGSTAR PORTFOLIO X-RAY

Portfolio X-Ray is an analytical tool that allows investors to dissect their portfolio and gain a clear view of their holdings and exposures.

Using Portfolio X-Ray, investors can evaluate their overall asset allocation and sector weightings as well as uncover concentrated positions, view the stock holdings behind their mutual funds, and measure performance against benchmarks and industry indexes. The Style Box plays a featured role in Portfolio X-Ray, which synthesizes an investor's holdings to present an aggregate picture of a portfolio's style exposures, as shown in **Exhibit 5.7**.

MORNINGSTAR CATEGORY

The Morningstar Style Box represents a snapshot in time of a fund or portfolio, but Morningstar also performs holdings-based analysis of long-term style trends. The Morningstar Category™ reflects the primary investment focus of the portfolio over the past three years. Categories

EXHIBIT 5.7. PORTFOLIO X-RAY

X-Ray Overview | X-Ray Details | X-Ray Interpreter | Stock Intersection

Asset Allocation | Holdings Detail ►►

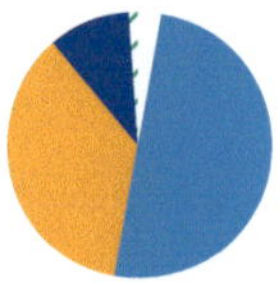

	Long%	Short%	Net%
Cash	3	3	3
US Stocks	50	0	50
Foreign Stocks	36	0	36
Bonds	10	0	10
Other	1	0	1
Not Classified	0	0	0
Total	**100**	**0**	**100**

☐ Show Short Position

Stock Style Diversification | Holdings Detail ►►

Valuation

Value	Core	Growth	*Size*
23	23	24	Large
5	8	10	Med
3	3	2	Small

Interest Rate Sensitivity

Ltd	Mod	Ext	*Credit Quality*
0	69	0	High
31	0	0	Med
0	0	0	Low

Not Classified 0.00% Not Classified 0.00%

Stock Sector | Holdings Details ►►

	Portfolio (% of Stocks)	S&P 500 (%)
Cyclical	**46.19**	**32.19**
Basic Materials	4.48	2.68
Consumer Cyclical	12.19	10.97
Financial Services	18.06	16.21
Real Estate	11.46	2.33
Sensitive	**32.13**	**41.40**
Communication Services	3.69	4.23
Energy	3.79	7.56
Industrials	11.89	11.03
Technology	12.76	18.58
Defensive	**21.68**	**26.41**
Consumer Defensive	6.28	9.49
Healthcare	13.56	13.75
Utilities	1.83	3.17
Not Classified	0.00	0.00

Stock Type | Holdings Detail ►►

	Portfolio (% of Domestic Stocks)	S&P 500 (%)
High Yield	**1.76**	4.78
Distressed	**2.34**	2.80
Hard Asset	**18.75**	6.98
Cyclical	**37.34**	40.48
Slow Growth	**15.67**	21.77
Classic Growth	**6.68**	7.70
Aggressive Growth	**9.16**	9.82
Speculative Growth	**3.68**	1.88
Not Classified	**4.62**	3.79

Fees & Expenses | Holdings Detail ►►

Average Mutual Fund Expense Ratio (%)	**0.30**
Expense Ratio of Similarly Weighted Hypothetical Portfolio (%)	**0.48**
Estimated Mutual Fund Expenses ($)	**1,506.88**
Total Sales Charges Paid ($)	**186.15**

World Regions | Holdings Detail ►►

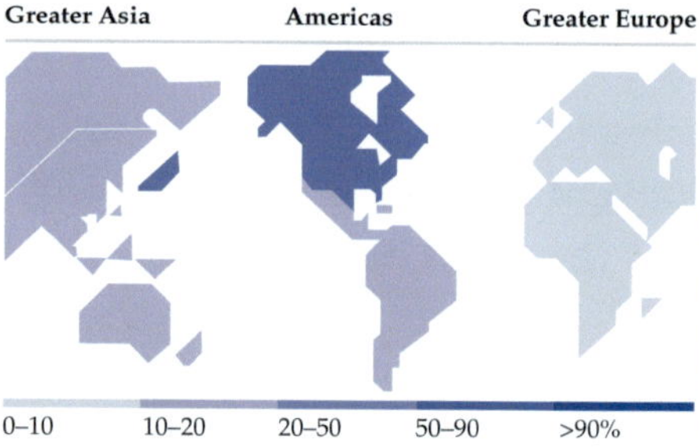

for equity funds can be based on style, country/regional exposure (e.g., Japan Stock), or economic sector focus (e.g., Specialty Technology).

In the United States, Morningstar uses 15 style-based categories. Nine of these categories are for diversified US equity funds, and the category names correspond to the nine squares of the Style Box (Large Value, Mid-Cap Blend, etc.). The remaining six style-based categories are used for diversified non-US equity funds (Foreign Large Value, Foreign Small/Mid Growth, etc.). Some of Morningstar's international operations also classify funds on the basis of style.

For further information on how Morningstar Categories are assigned and maintained, see Appendix B.5, "Morningstar Category Assignment and Maintenance Process."

MORNINGSTAR STYLE TRAIL

The Style Trail tool leverages the Style Box methodology and holdings-based data to offer investors a historical view of the movement of a portfolio over time. This view can yield insights into the way a fund's portfolio has been managed over time and whether the approach has remained consistent.

To illustrate, in **Exhibit 5.8**, the fund's style appears to have drifted significantly over time (the size of each circle indicates its age, with

EXHIBIT 5.8. MORNINGSTAR STYLE TRAIL

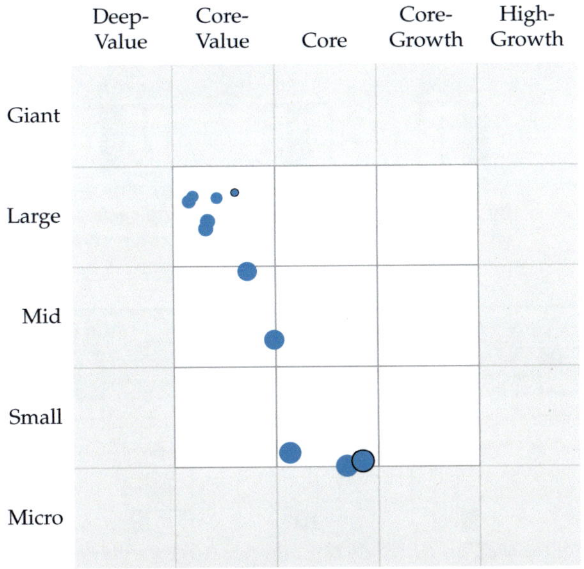

the oldest portfolio represented by the smallest circle and the more recent by the largest), from value to growth and from the stocks of larger companies to small-caps. Although such changes might be consonant with the investment approach, they would probably stimulate follow-up research to ensure that the fund was not deviating from its intended objective and role in the portfolio.

MORNINGSTAR STYLE INDEXES

The Morningstar Style Index family consists of 16 indexes that track the US equity market by capitalization and investment style to create an integrated system (**Exhibit 5.9**). The indexes were built using a

EXHIBIT 5.9. OVERVIEW OF THE STYLE INDEX FAMILY

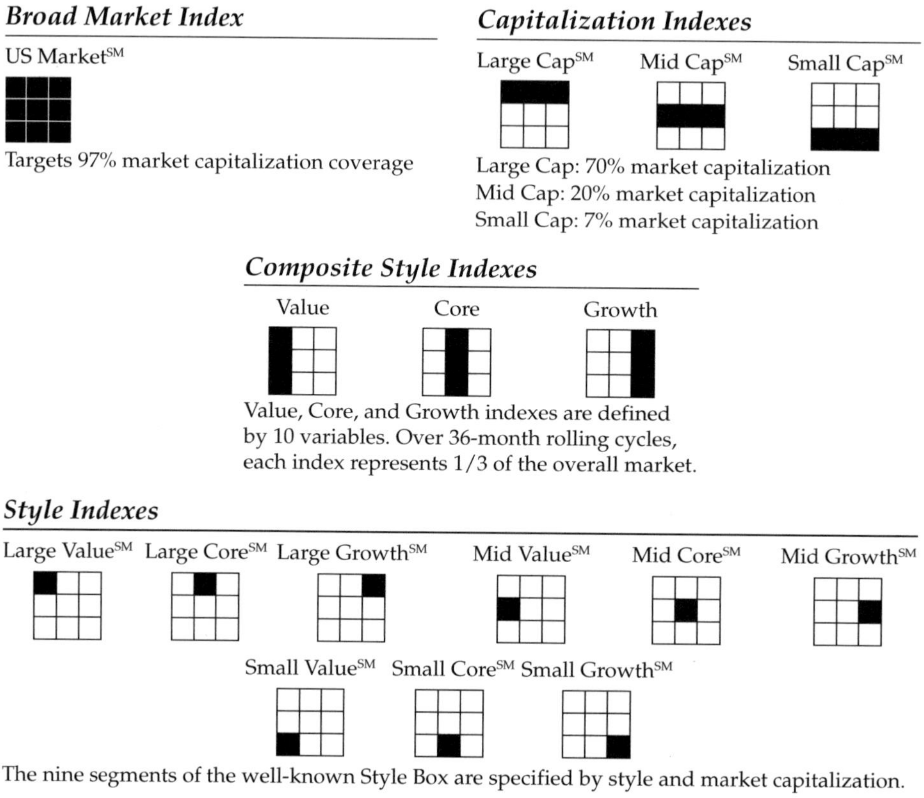

comprehensive and nonoverlapping approach based on the methodology of the Morningstar Style Box and thus represent an additional tool that investors can use to compare and benchmark investments.

Index constituents are weighted according to their free float of shares outstanding. To help ensure that index turnover reflects significant events, stocks are reclassified in terms of style or capitalization only if they move sufficiently beyond the breakpoint between styles or capitalizations (known as the "buffer zone").

THE STYLE BOX AND FACTOR MODELS

In "Holdings-Based and Returns-Based Style Models" (Kaplan 2003), one finds a primer for combining the holdings-based Morningstar equity Style Box approach with multi-factor asset-pricing models, such as the Fama–French model.

To illustrate, we can use the Morningstar Style Box methodology to construct a set of four reference portfolios: large-cap value, large-cap growth, small-cap value, and small-cap growth. Using these reference portfolios, we can implement the Fama–French model as follows:

$$r_{Ft} = \alpha + \beta_Q r_{Mt} + \gamma_x (r_{LVt} + r_{SVt} - r_{LGt} - r_{SGt}) + \gamma_y (r_{SVt} + r_{SGt} - r_{LVt} - r_{LGt}) + \varepsilon_t$$

where

r_{Ft} = total return on the fund in month t

r_{Mt} = total return on the equity market portfolio minus return on cash in month t

γ_x = a parameter that measures the fund's value/growth orientation

γ_y = a parameter that measures the fund's size orientation

r_{LVt} = total return on the large-cap value reference portfolio in month t

r_{LGt} = total return on the large-cap growth reference portfolio in month t

r_{SVt} = total return on the small-cap value reference portfolio in month t

r_{SGt} = total return on the small-cap growth reference portfolio in month t

α = intercept

β_Q = coefficient on portfolio Q (Q = LV, LG, SV, SG)

ε_t = error term in month t

APPENDIX A.5. HOLDINGS-BASED VS. RETURNS-BASED ANALYSIS

Although style analysis is widely regarded as a valuable exercise, there is still considerable debate about how style should be measured. There are two main approaches to style analysis: holdings based and returns based.

HOLDINGS-BASED ANALYSIS

Holdings-based style analysis is a "bottom-up" approach in which the characteristics of a fund over a period are derived from the characteristics of the securities it contains at various points in time over the period. The choice of characteristics depends on the purpose of the analysis. If the purpose is to create a customized benchmark consisting of a portfolio of indexes or to decompose the portfolio into a set of asset classes, the only security characteristic needed is index or asset class membership. If the purpose is to describe a portfolio in terms of a set of quantitative style characteristics, such as size and value/growth orientation, the prescribed characteristics of each security need to be calculated and then aggregated to the portfolio level.

Holdings-based style analysis requires two sets of data. First, we need a security database that contains the characteristics of each security in the investable universe of the funds being analyzed. Second, we need a record of the security holdings of each fund being analyzed. Each database must contain the requisite data for each period studied.

The databases needed to perform holdings-based style analysis are expensive to obtain and keep up to date. Thus, there are only a handful of investment research firms that have the needed datasets and perform holdings-based style analysis.

RETURNS-BASED ANALYSIS

Sharpe (1988, 1992) introduced a low-cost alternative to holdings-based style analysis—namely, returns-based style analysis. Sharpe's approach is to regress a fund's historical returns against the returns of a set of passively constructed reference portfolios, each reference portfolio representing an asset class or an investment style. The coefficients on the reference portfolio returns are constrained to be non-negative and sum to 1 so that they represent a long-only portfolio of passive investments. This portfolio serves as the fund's custom benchmark.

Sharpe's model made style analysis readily available to anyone who could obtain historical returns data on the portfolio being analyzed and on passive indexes. Owing to the importance of style analysis and the relative inexpensiveness of returns data, Sharpe's model quickly became popular among institutional investors and consultants. Several firms developed software packages for both the institutional market and the adviser market to perform returns-based style analysis.

Most of these software packages create plots of equity style characteristics of funds. To do so, they first assign a point in x, y space to each reference portfolio that represents a specific equity style, such as large-cap value. They then generate a plot point for the fund in question by taking a weighted average of the plot points of the reference portfolios, using the results of returns-based style analysis for the weights.

WEIGHING THE TWO APPROACHES

Morningstar has long been a proponent of holdings-based style analysis but recognizes that there may be situations where returns-based style analysis can also be helpful. Because the two approaches are so different, it is important to understand how the models work in order to correctly interpret the results.

Two separate Morningstar studies evaluated the results and assumptions of each approach.

Each study's author ran holdings-based and returns-based analysis on a large set of portfolios and compared the results. The first study (Kaplan 2003) used both methods to produce *x*- and *y*-coordinates for value/growth orientation and size. The author used Morningstar's 10-factor style model and plotted each fund's coordinates on the Morningstar Style Box. He then measured the closeness of the returns-based plot and the holdings-based plot for each portfolio. The second study (Rekenthaler, Gambera, and Charlson 2004) compared the style breakdowns produced by each method. The style breakdown is the percentage of assets attributed to each style (e.g., small value, small growth, and mid-cap value). This second study used the Russell style indexes as a baseline.

Kaplan (2003) demonstrated that the accuracy of returns-based style analysis varies for different styles of portfolios. For example, returns-based style analysis usually results in plot points that are similar to holdings-based plots for large-cap and value-oriented portfolios. However, Kaplan found significant variation between the two methods for small-cap, mid-cap, and growth-oriented funds. Furthermore, he demonstrated that descriptive statistics (such as R^2) from the returns-based model can sometimes be misleading, implying more accuracy than is present.

Either approach can produce inaccurate results if exposed to certain flaws in the application design or certain limitations in the data. These are practical concerns rather than flaws in the method. Kaplan (2003) argued that most returns-based style applications impose unnecessary constraints that act as fences, keeping the style results within certain boundaries, which makes it difficult to detect more-aggressive positions, such as deep value and micro-cap. Also, the limited availability of data on derivatives often makes holdings-based style analysis less effective for funds with substantial positions in derivatives.

Rekenthaler et al. (2004) addressed a different question—namely, the timeliness of the models' results. Some argue that holdings-based style analysis can be stale, because portfolios are not always available on a monthly basis. Others argue that returns-based style analysis can be stale, because it requires a long string of historical monthly returns. The authors found that a holdings-based style analysis of a year-old portfolio produces better results than a returns-based analysis using "current" data. In other words, a snapshot that is 12 months old is more accurate than a 36-month average. Furthermore, holdings-based analysis is more stable and consistent over time than returns-based analysis and thus provides a better estimate of the portfolio's future style and risk.

Investors should also consider the following characteristics of these models:

- Because returns-based style analysis requires 20–36 months of performance, this approach cannot be used for portfolios that are brand new or to detect style changes over shorter periods.
- Returns-based style analysis can be used to validate the completeness and accuracy of reported portfolio holdings. If the returns-based analysis is considerably different from the holdings-based analysis, it may indicate that the portfolio manager is not disclosing all of his or her holdings.
- Returns-based style analysis is dependent on the choice of benchmark indexes. Holdings-based style analysis is dependent on the choice of style framework.
- Holdings-based style analysis is transparent. Because stocks and portfolios use the same style framework, portfolio managers can see how each holding contributes to their average portfolio style and can take action if the portfolio's style is drifting from its target.

The relationship between stock style and fund style can be seen in the Morningstar Ownership Zone, a tool that plots each holding on the Morningstar Style Box.

- Returns-based style analysis is most accurate when the correlations between the benchmark indexes are low. If the indexes have performed in a highly correlated fashion, it is harder for the model to detect distinct style patterns in the total returns.

APPENDIX B.5. MORNINGSTAR CATEGORY ASSIGNMENT AND MAINTENANCE PROCESS

Morningstar reviews category assignments semi-annually, incorporating all portfolio data over the prior three years up to the most recent quarter-end. The process is partly quantitative: A program calculates the three-year averages for various statistics and makes a recommendation about the appropriate category for the portfolio. The process is also qualitative: Morningstar's manager research analyst team will review the suggestions from the quantitative program and, on the basis of their unique knowledge of the funds, will make a recommendation about whether the changes should be overruled or upheld. These results are then communicated to the fund company.

Funds are assigned to style-based categories on the basis of their three-year average raw X and raw Y scores. The three-year average is the simple average of three 12-month averages, using the portfolio files received over that period. The Morningstar categories, in turn, serve as the peer groups that are used for purposes of assigning the Morningstar Rating™ to funds, more commonly known as the "Star Rating" (see **Exhibit 5.10**).

EXHIBIT 5.10. THE MORNINGSTAR RATING

The Morningstar Rating We provide Morningstar ratings for funds (based on historical risk and returns) and stocks (based on our fair value estimates).	★★★★★ ★★★★ ★★★ ★★ ★

When there are fewer funds in certain investment styles, Morningstar may support only two categories across the value/growth spectrum. In these cases, funds with three-year average raw X scores below 150 are placed in the value category and funds with three-year average raw X scores greater than or equal to 150 are placed in the growth category.

Some Morningstar operations may use discretion or buffering mechanisms during the Morningstar Category review process. These methods ensure that a fund does not undergo a category change unless it has exhibited a strong and sustained shift into a new investment style. That is, a fund may not necessarily experience a category change if the three-year average has landed just over a breakpoint by a small amount. (These buffering mechanisms are for category placement only and do not apply to Style Box assignments.)

APPENDIX C.5. MORNINGSTAR FIXED-INCOME STYLE BOX

In addition to the Morningstar Equity Style Box, Morningstar also classifies bond funds in its Morningstar Fixed-Income Style Box. Like the Equity Style Box, the Fixed-Income Style Box has two key dimensions: interest rate sensitivity (limited, moderate, extensive) and credit quality (high, medium, low). The nine possible combinations of these characteristics correspond to the nine squares of the Fixed-Income Style Box; quality is displayed along the vertical axis and interest rate sensitivity along the horizontal axis.

HORIZONTAL AXIS: INTEREST RATE SENSITIVITY

Prior to October 2009, US taxable-bond funds domiciled in the United States with durations of 3.5 years or less were considered short term (having limited sensitivity to interest rate changes); durations of more than 3.5 years but less than 6.0 years were considered intermediate term (having moderate sensitivity to interest rate changes); and durations of more than 6.0 years were considered long term (having extensive sensitivity to interest rate changes). In October

2009, Morningstar moved from these static breakpoints to dynamic breakpoints.

On a monthly basis, Morningstar calculates duration breakpoints based on the effective duration of the Morningstar Core Bond Index (MCBI).

- Limited: 25% to 75% of MCBI
- Moderate: 75% to 125% of MCBI
- Extensive: 125% of MCBI (no upper limit on long-term durations)

Non-US taxable-bond funds domiciled in the United States use static duration breakpoints, including US-domiciled funds in the World Bond category and the Emerging-Markets Bond category.

- Limited: ≤ 3.5 years
- Moderate: > 3.5 and ≤ 6.0 years
- Extensive: > 6.0 years

Municipal-bond funds domiciled in the United States use static duration breakpoints.

- Limited: ≤ 4.5 years
- Moderate: > 4.5 and ≤ 7.0 years
- Extensive: > 7.0 years

VERTICAL AXIS: CREDIT QUALITY

Historically, Morningstar followed the industry practice of reporting the average credit rating of a bond portfolio by computing a weighted average of ratings on the basis of data provided by fund companies.

However, because default rates tend to rise at a nearly geometric pace between the lowest grades (a mathematical property called convexity), this method systematically understated the average default rate of a bond portfolio. For example, for US corporate bonds, the spread in default rates between CCC- and BBB-rated bonds was more than 21 times that of the default-rate spread between BBB and AAA bonds. Yet, the conventional averaging method assumes that these spreads are equal.

To see the impact of this approach, consider a portfolio of 90% AAA bonds and 10% CCC bonds. According to the conventional method, the average credit rating of this portfolio is AA. However, the average default rate for this portfolio is that of BB bonds.

To correct this bias, Morningstar takes the convexity of default-rate curves into account when calculating the average credit rating of a portfolio. The first step is to map the grades of a portfolio's constituents into relative default rates using a convex curve. Next, average the resulting default rates on a weighted basis (rather than the grades) to come up with an average default rate for the portfolio. Finally, using the same convex curve, Morningstar maps the resulting average default rate back into a grade. For example, a portfolio of 90% AAA bonds and 10% CCC bonds will have an average credit rating of BB under this new methodology.

On the basis of the following breakpoints, Morningstar maps the calculated average asset-weighted letter credit rating (see Appendix A.5) for all portfolios on the vertical axis of the Style Box:

1. Low credit quality: asset-weighted average credit rating is less than BBB.
2. Medium credit quality: asset-weighted average credit rating is less than AA but greater than or equal to BBB.
3. High credit quality: asset-weighted average credit rating is AA or higher.

REFERENCES

Kaplan, Paul D. 2003. "Holdings-Based and Returns-Based Style Models." Morningstar Research Report (June): http://corporate.morningstar.com/ES/documents/MethodologyDocuments/ResearchPapers/Holdings-basedAndReturns-basedStyleModels_PK.pdf.

Rekenthaler, John, Michele Gambera, and Joshua Charlson. 2004. "Estimating Portfolio Style in U.S. Equity Funds: A Comparative Study of Portfolio-Based Fundamental Style Analysis and Returns-Based Style Analysis." Morningstar Research Report (25 February): http://corporate.morningstar.com/no/documents/MethodologyDocuments/ResearchPapers/EstimatingPortfolioStyle_MGJRJC.pdf.

Sharpe, William F. 1988, 1992. "Asset Allocation: Management Style and Performance Measurement." *Journal of Portfolio Management*, vol. 18, no. 2 (Winter): 7–19.

PART II

CASE STUDIES AND MANAGER INTERVIEWS

6. GIC—MANAGING SINGAPORE'S FINANCIAL RESERVES FOR THE LONG TERM

Darius Liu, CFA
Tham Chiew Kit
Leslie Teo, PhD, CFA

GIC was incorporated in 1981 as a private company wholly owned by the Singapore government to preserve and enhance the international purchasing power of Singapore's financial reserves.

When GIC was founded, Singapore was a young nation. Since its independence in 1965, the Singapore government's pragmatic economic policies and prudent fiscal stance have resulted in a rapid growth of Singapore's reserves through a sustained balance of payment and budget surpluses year after year.

Indeed, by the late 1970s, this pool of reserves had grown to a size above what would be required to meet the obligations of Singapore's currency board or the resources needed by the central bank to manage the floating parity of the Singapore dollar. It was decided that a portion of the reserves would be managed by GIC as long-term investments, separate from the reserves parked within the central bank. GIC was tasked to generate good returns from capital appreciation over the long term by investing in longer-term, higher-yielding assets. This pool of reserves was initially intended as Singapore's "rainy day fund"—a safeguard against unforeseen shocks that may buffet Singapore's economy. A portion of the returns from the reserves managed by GIC also serves to supplement Singapore's annual budget and can be spent or invested for the benefit of Singaporeans.

6.1. GIC'S MANDATE—DEFINING SUCCESS FOR GIC

GIC's client—the Singapore government, represented by the Ministry of Finance—has given GIC a mandate to *achieve good long-term returns over global inflation, within specified risk limits.*[1] Three aspects of this mandate are important to appreciate:

1. GIC's mandate incorporates a *real return* target. This ensures that the purchasing power of the reserves does not get eroded by inflation over time.
2. The emphasis on *long-term returns* aligns GIC's investment horizon with that of the client and allows GIC to keep a focus on long-term returns without having to manage the portfolio in response to short-term market fluctuations. Practically, the performance of GIC is measured on a total portfolio basis, over a 20-year horizon.
3. GIC's portfolio is managed to maximize expected return while *minimizing the likelihood of large losses that may lead to permanent impairment.*[2] Consistent with this, one of the risk parameters of the portfolio is defined in terms of how the portfolio's value can fall over a period. This risk parameter, along with other risk constraints such as the active risk budget, are designed for consistency with GIC's long-term orientation. Later sections of this article will provide more detail on these risk parameters.

Additionally, GIC's client has specified a Reference Portfolio (RP) for GIC. This RP comprises 65% global equities and 35% global bonds (65:35) and constitutes a generally accepted alternative for GIC that is consistent with the client's risk tolerance. That said, the RP is not a short-term performance or investment benchmark for GIC.

Through a disciplined investment process within a well-structured investment framework coupled with a robust risk management process, both the client and GIC expect the GIC portfolio to deliver on its mandate (points 1, 2, and 3). In doing so, both the client and GIC would expect the GIC portfolio to also outperform the RP over a 20-year time horizon. It is to this investment framework we now turn.

---

[1]Singapore MOF policy page: http://www.mof.gov.sg/Policies/Our-Nations-Reserves/Section-I-What-comprises-the-reserves-and-who-manages-them; GIC Annual Reports.
[2]GIC Annual Report, 2015/2016.

6.2. GIC'S INVESTMENT FRAMEWORK

GIC's investment framework has evolved over time as the organization—and Singapore as a whole—have grown and developed. In the early years, GIC's investment stance was conservative, with a focus on building a strong investment organization. The portfolio had more bonds and predominantly invested in publicly traded instruments. As GIC's investment capabilities grew, more markets and financial assets were included in the portfolio. The risk and return profile of the GIC portfolio also shifted to reflect a greater emphasis on long-term, intergenerational returns over shorter-term liquidity needs, as shown in **Exhibit 6.1**.

In 2012, GIC embarked on a comprehensive review of its investment framework, in response to the growing complexity of managing a multi-asset, multi-strategy portfolio in an increasingly challenging investment environment. This "new investment framework" is designed to achieve clarity on

1. the different drivers of return to the GIC Portfolio;
2. the horizon over which they pay off; and
3. how to achieve strong governance around investment decisions and attribution of returns.

EXHIBIT 6.1 MAJOR CHANGES TO GIC'S INVESTMENT FRAMEWORK

FIRST TWO DECADES	2000s	2013
Conservative Stance	Shift to an Endowment Approach	Focus on Long-Term Drivers of Returns
Focused on building organizational capabilities	Greater tolerance for risk and lower need for liquidity	Introduction of a Reference Portfolio
Conservative asset allocation focused on liquid assets	Increased allocation to private markets and emerging markets	A more targeted Policy Portfolio to harvest long-term returns
Venturing into Asia		Augmented with an Active Portfollo of skill-based strategies
Beginning exposures to real estate and private equity		

The architecture of the GIC portfolio (represented in **Exhibit 6.2**) neatly encapsulates these three aforementioned design considerations. Within this construct, the GIC Portfolio can be conceptually divided into two components.

A) *The Policy Portfolio (PP).* The Policy Portfolio is constructed to harvest systematic risk premia from core asset classes over the long term. For GIC, six core asset classes have been identified: developed market equities, emerging market equities, nominal bonds and cash, inflation-linked bonds, private equity, and real estate. Diversification across these asset classes serves to improve the risk–return profile of the PP as a whole.

   Because the PP is structured to capture time-varying, long-term risk premia arising from structural changes in the global environment, the PP is not intended to be adjusted frequently in response to market cycles. Nevertheless, the PP is reviewed regularly to determine whether any changes to the mix are needed.

EXHIBIT 6.2 GIC'S INVESTMENT FRAMEWORK

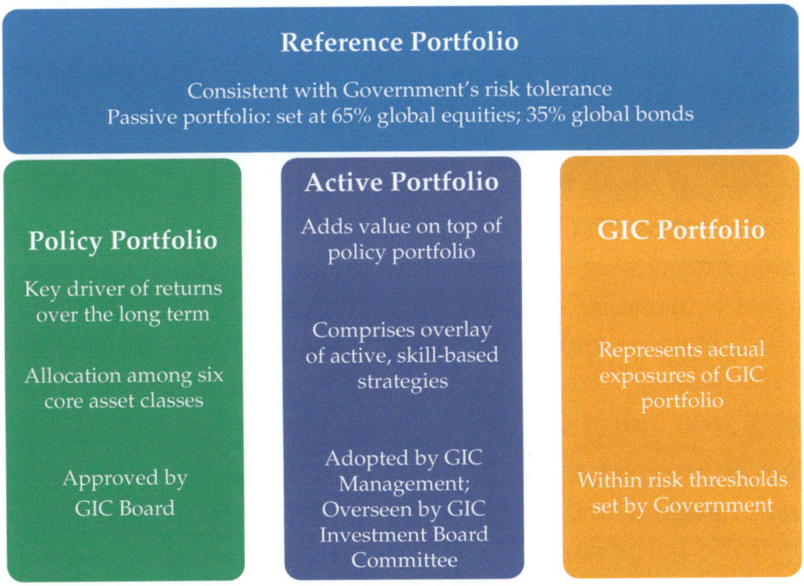

Concurrently, a disciplined rebalancing regime serves to keep this asset mix steady over time and is expected to contribute to good performance in the long run.

From the governance perspective, the PP's mix is recommended by GIC's management and approved by GIC's Board. The performance of the PP is evaluated over a 20-year timeframe.

B) *The Active Portfolio (AP).* While the Policy Portfolio, on its own, serves to reap systematic long-term risk premia, GIC recognizes the need to add value on top of the PP, to increase the likelihood of achieving GIC's overall mandate. This is especially pertinent given more muted prospects for asset returns over the next 10–20 years, as compared with returns from the 1980s to the 2000s. Indeed, GIC expects the prospective real return from both the PP and RP to be lower due to unprecedented low interest rates, modest growth prospects globally, and high asset valuations. The contribution of the AP to GIC's total return is thus expected to grow in importance.

In essence, the AP is made up of GIC's entire suite of active strategies, each targeting its own separate stream of excess return over their own specific performance benchmarks. One key difference between the AP and PP is the time horizon for each portfolio. While the PP reaps long-term risk premia (over 20 years or more), the AP is made up of active strategies that generate value add over 5–7 years from excess return streams that have very low correlation with PP asset class returns.

As a whole, the AP is designed to add value above the PP. This is achieved through GIC's "cost of capital" (CoC) system—an integral part of our overall investment framework. The GIC Investment Board is tasked with the oversight of the AP. More details on the CoC system, as well as the principles underlying the construction of the AP and selection of active strategies, are outlined in greater detail later in this chapter.

C) ***The GIC Portfolio.*** The GIC Portfolio represents the actual investment holdings of GIC at any point in time. The return of the GIC Portfolio is the sum of the PP return and the total value added generated by the AP above the PP. It is this total portfolio return, over a 20-year horizon, that GIC is held accountable to. GIC's focus on long-term total portfolio return is worth emphasizing—while GIC makes individual investments on the basis of a favorable risk–reward profile after taking into account available information, we acknowledge that all investments carry risks. There will inevitably be some investments that do not turn out as well as we had hoped, and we recognize that losses on certain investments will happen. GIC takes every decline in the value of individual investments very seriously and aims to learn from every such occurrence. However, we believe that maintaining our long-term orientation, taking calculated risks, and running a diversified portfolio with a disciplined rebalancing process give us the best chance of achieving good long-term real returns for the portfolio as a whole.

As previously mentioned, the RP also forms part of the investment framework, notwithstanding that it does not form part of the GIC Portfolio per se. The RP serves as a passive portfolio that is consistent with the client's risk tolerance. The RP, by construction, will be more volatile than the GIC Portfolio, which is more diversified.

The overall architecture of the GIC Portfolio (illustrated in **Exhibit 6.3**) clearly sets out, at a broad level, the different return streams that GIC aims to harvest and allows for a clear delineation of responsibility across various parts of GIC around the associated investment decisions. Importantly, the separation between passive returns (beta) and active, skill-based value added (alpha) enables a greater level of understanding and management of the return and risk of the GIC Portfolio as a whole.

The discussion that follows will provide more detail on the principles underlying the construction of the PP and AP and illustrate why these are important in the context of the overall GIC Portfolio.

EXHIBIT 6.3 THE ARCHITECTURE OF THE GIC PORTFOLIO

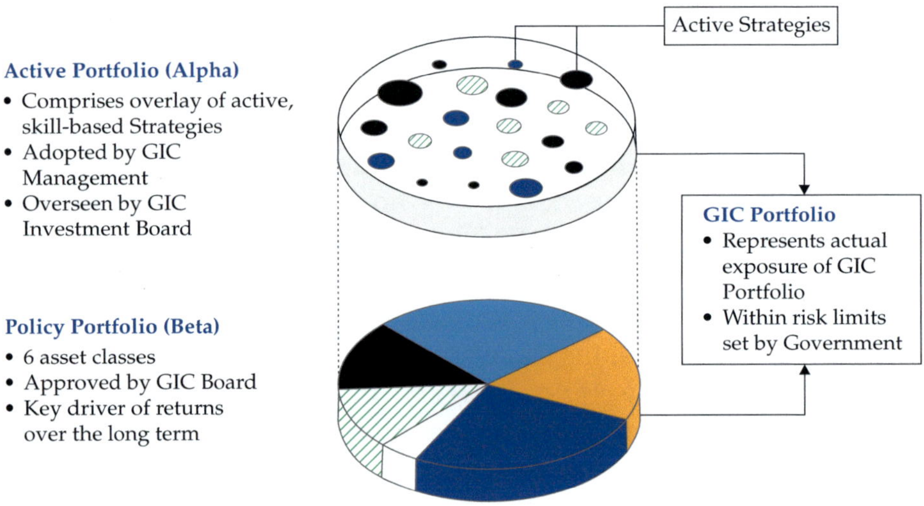

6.3. THE POLICY PORTFOLIO

To recap, the aim of the Policy Portfolio is to harvest long-term systematic risk premia via exposure to core asset classes. In terms of time horizon, the PP is aligned with the client's overall goal of achieving good real returns over 20 years, subject to risk constraints. The PP represents the bulk of the GIC portfolio's overall risk. As such, any changes to asset class weights in the PP are approved by the Board, upon recommendation by GIC management.

The following principles govern the construction of the PP. This methodology allows the asset classes in the PP to be put together in a mix that aims to maximize the chance of delivering good real returns over the long term.

1. *Robustness.* The future is inherently uncertain, and both GIC's management and Board recognize the need to have a degree of humility when it comes to predicting the behavior of the markets and the macroeconomic environment. As such, the PP is designed to meet the client's mandate across a range of plausible market scenarios. For a particular outcome, the PP may *not* be the portfolio

that gives the highest return. However, given a set of plausible market outcomes, the PP is designed to achieve reasonably good real returns regardless of which specific outcome eventually transpires. While we acknowledge that it would not be practical to take into account every single *possible* scenario, we believe that this consideration of robustness relative to an appropriate set of *plausible* scenarios is a prudent approach in a world where the future is uncertain. In addition, GIC employs stress tests based on a variety of extreme scenarios to determine the impact of tail events on the portfolio. The results of these analyses form a valuable input into the portfolio construction process.

2. *Diversified.* GIC's PP is constructed to achieve a good degree of diversification, to benefit from the distinct characteristics of each asset class in the policy mix. For instance, the GIC portfolio aims to generate good long-term returns via exposure to growth assets such as public and private equity, but it also offers protection from downside risk via exposure to defensive assets, such as high-quality nominal bonds.

   By definition, a diversified portfolio such as the PP will underperform more-concentrated portfolios in certain scenarios. The last five-year period is a case in point—because of the strong bull run in developed market equities over this period, particularly in the United States, the PP underperformed portfolios with a larger allocation to developed market equities (such as the RP, for instance). However, this same PP is expected to outperform in a bear market. Over the long term, a well-diversified portfolio provides the best mix of safety and growth and offers the best chance of contributing to the fulfillment of GIC's mandate.

3. *Good long-term return potential.* The PP must be constructed such that, on a forward-looking basis, the portfolio has good long-term return potential. In practice, this requires the PP's asset classes to be chosen carefully—only those asset classes that are able to offer good long-term returns (even if they are time varying over shorter horizons) should be included in the PP. The only exceptions to this principle are defensive asset classes, which are included to bolster

the robustness of the PP as a whole as well as to ensure the PP's risk characteristics are within pre-specified limits.

These long-term risk premia that the PP aims to capture generally stem from investor risk aversion and a desire for liquidity, supported by corporate or government revenues. Long-term returns are also affected by secular forces, starting valuations, trends in investor behavior, changes to market structures, and a tendency for asset values to revert to some "equilibrium" level. In GIC's regular review of the PP mix, these factors are carefully analyzed to determine how the prospective long-term returns from each asset class are affected and the attendant impact on the optimal PP mix. GIC's management is also constantly scanning the investment environment to determine if any other asset classes should be included in the PP. For example, high-yield credit had been considered as a potential asset class in the PP, but after a thorough analysis, GIC concluded that high-yield credit did not sufficiently meet the criteria for inclusion in the PP.

4. *Adherence to risk limits.* The risk constraints imposed on the GIC portfolio affect the construction of the PP. This is because the PP is the main contributor of risk to the GIC portfolio. By including some exposure to defensive assets, such as nominal bonds and inflation-linked bonds, the overall risk of the PP can be reduced.

The process of selecting asset class weights in the PP invariably involves a combination of quantitative analysis and qualitative professional judgment. The eventual PP mix that is adopted depends heavily on ex ante return and risk projections for each asset class, which are modeled based on a forward-looking assessment with some guidance from history. Using a suite of forward-looking scenarios, candidate portfolios are constructed and tested against the criteria outlined above. The final PP is selected based on a balance of risk factors, robustness and acceptable return, subject to the market capacity of each asset class. **Exhibit 6.4** provides a conceptual illustration of the PP construction process.

EXHIBIT 6.4 THE PP CONSTRUCTION PROCESS—A CONCEPTUAL ILLUSTRATION

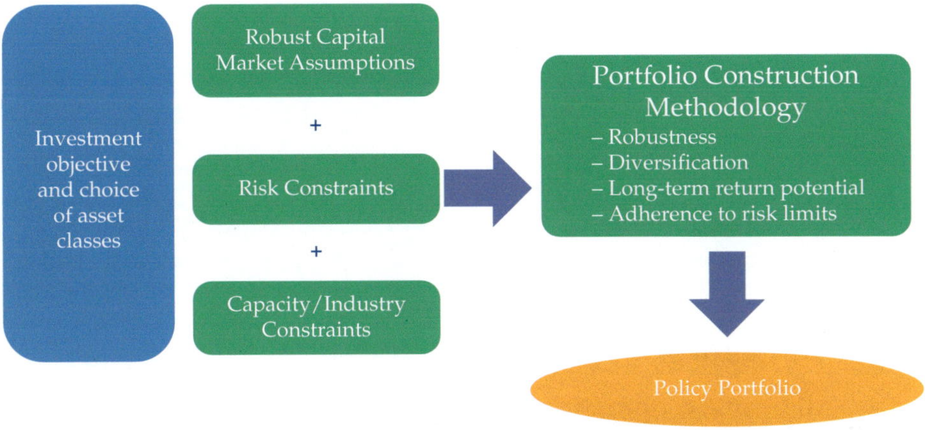

6.4. THE ACTIVE PORTFOLIO

As outlined earlier, the Active Portfolio serves to add additional return above that of the PP. The construction of the AP is governed by a risk budget set by the Board, which determines the maximum extent to which the AP can deviate from the PP. In addition, the GIC Investment Board oversees the AP as a whole.

In GIC's investment framework, each active strategy replaces part of the passive exposure in the PP with a skill-based, value-adding investment opportunity. An easy way to understand this is to think of part of the PP being sold and the cash raised is then passed on to an active strategy to fund its investment activities. This active strategy is then expected to generate a return that is higher than its "cost of capital"—that is, what GIC would have otherwise received from the passive investments that were sold to fund the strategy plus other premia for additional risk taken.

Put another way, the CoC approach to funding active strategies aims to separate the systematic risks in each strategy (represented by the CoC, i.e., returns of the passive assets that are "sold" to fund the strategy plus premia for additional risks taken) from the returns attributable to the skill of the strategy team (represented by the value added above the CoC). This "risk-matching" approach helps to ensure that the active strategies will not have a significant impact on the risk characteristics of the portfolio as a whole.

In this construct, the following design principles govern the construction of the AP and selection and sizing of the constituent active strategies.

1. *Ability to add value to the GIC portfolio.* An active strategy is deemed to be ex ante *accretive* to GIC if its return is expected to cover:

    - the return of the passive assets used to fund the strategy;
    - all business operating costs and fees; and
    - hedging costs, if any.

    In addition, the expected positive risk-adjusted added value of a strategy must compare favorably with other strategies in order to justify an allocation within the AP.

2. *Scalability of each strategy.* Strategies within the AP need to be reasonably scalable before being given an allocation in the AP, even if they have superior value-adding potential on a percentage basis. This is true for the following reasons:

    - The total size of the GIC Portfolio is large—well over US$100 billion. A strategy needs to be able to scale to a certain size before it can make an appreciable impact on the GIC Portfolio's total return.
    - If a strategy's maximum size is too small, it will be difficult to justify the investment in human resources and infrastructure required to run the strategy.

3. *Diversification and risk characteristics.* As a result of the CoC system of funding active strategies, the AP as a whole should be, in essence, a collection of uncorrelated streams of alpha return.

The AP thus should not only be diversified but also have a low correlation with the PP.

Continuous robust evaluation of the active strategies (and the AP as a whole) is vital in ensuring that the AP achieves its outperformance objective while keeping within the prescribed risk limits. This is especially so given that the evaluation timeframe of active strategies is shorter than that for the PP, ranging from five to seven years on average, depending on the nature of each strategy.

Both the strategy teams and GIC management need to be vigilant to changes in market structure, macroeconomic trends, and investor behavior that could render the investment thesis of a strategy invalid. In such instances, there are established processes to downsize or close down such strategies and redeploy the capital to other strategies with stronger value-adding potential. A monitoring process is also in place to alert the strategy teams and management to fundamental changes to the risk characteristics of a strategy so that appropriate changes can be made to how the strategy's risks are being monitored and managed.

In other instances, although the investment thesis and market opportunity for a particular strategy may remain promising, GIC may not have the required expertise in-house to harvest these alpha streams. In such scenarios, a choice can be made to use external managers to access the returns in the strategy. As a general principle, the choice between internal and external managers for any given strategy is made objectively based on the "best sourcing" principle net of costs and fees.

The principles that guide the construction and constant reevaluation of the AP ensure that the AP continues to play a key role in contributing to the total return of the GIC Portfolio without adding to the risk of the GIC Portfolio in a significant way. **Exhibit 6.5** provides a stylized illustration of the benefits the AP can bring to the total portfolio. The addition of alpha that is uncorrelated with the PP gives the total portfolio superior risk–return characteristics. The alpha–beta separation afforded by this investment framework also allows a more accurate

EXHIBIT 6.5 THE BENEFITS OF ADDING ALPHA

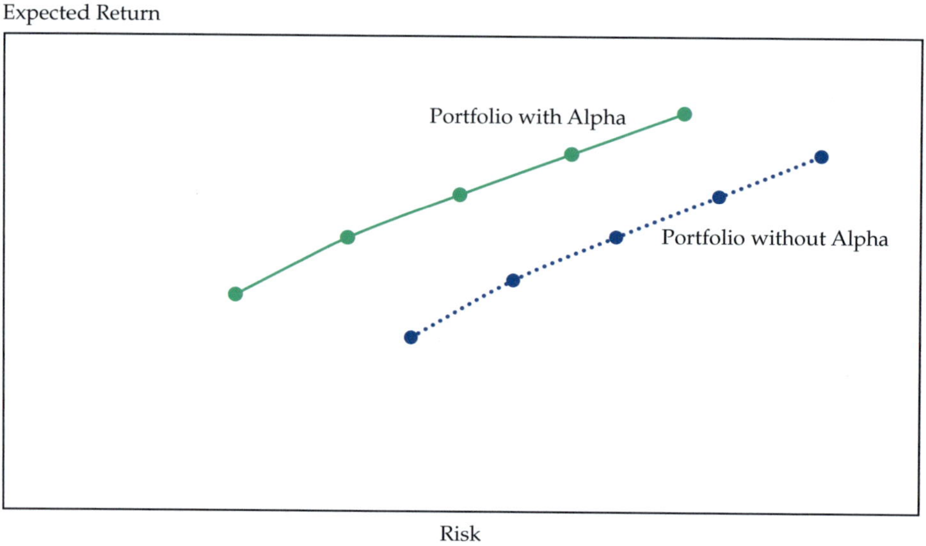

Notes: The dots on each efficient frontier represent different allocations of both public and private market risk assets. The corresponding dots on the frontier for the "Portfolio with Alpha" result from the addition of an AP with zero correlation with the PP. Each AP is assumed to represent 70% of the size of the total portfolio. In all cases, addition of the AP shifts the efficient frontier upwards and to the left, representing better expected returns for a given level of risk.

attribution of return across various strategy teams in GIC, as well as a more granular understanding of the various sources of return across the portfolio.

6.5. GIC'S STRENGTHS

Although a strong and robust investment framework is critical to GIC's ability to meet our client's objective of achieving good long-term real returns, GIC recognizes that a framework is useful only if it is complemented by good processes, policies, and people. The following investment beliefs and aspects of GIC's organizational culture serve to complement GIC's investment framework and allow GIC to access investment opportunities not commonly accessible to other investors.

1. *Long-term investment perspective.* Being able to invest with a long-term horizon is a key advantage GIC possesses. The long-term and diversified nature of the GIC portfolio, coupled with sound governance and risk management processes, allow GIC to ride through both short-term market volatility as well as more severe market crises. Our investment framework and processes also allow GIC to take advantage of opportunities that may arise from market downturns, through taking a contrarian stance in the face of short-term sentiment to reap long-term risk premia. The fact that GIC represents a large pool of stable, patient capital has also made us an attractive investor of choice.

2. *Clear governance structure.* The clear governance structure afforded by GIC's investment framework provides clear lines of accountability throughout the organization. Clarity of roles allows every professional in GIC to focus on building deep expertise, with the assurance that good performance will be accurately attributed and rewarded.

3. *Robust risk management framework and a risk-conscious culture.* GIC's risk management framework lays out appropriate accountability and responsibility parameters for risk taking at all levels of the organization, from the Board down to individual members of investment teams. A dedicated risk and performance management department conducts regular monitoring of performance and risk to ensure adherence to defined risk thresholds, as well as highlighting portfolio behaviors that are inconsistent with stated risk and return assumptions. Processes are likewise in place to monitor and mitigate legal, regulatory compliance, infrastructure, operational, and people risk. GIC aims to continually reinforce a risk-conscious culture at all levels of the organization, as we believe that such a mindset forms the bedrock of an effective risk management framework that will effectively contribute to good portfolio outcomes.

4. *Culture of collaboration.* As a multi-asset investor, GIC has an expertise in investing across a wide range of asset classes. Crucially, GIC has developed a culture of collaboration where there are processes for teams from different asset classes to pool resources and

invest synergistically, for instance, across the capital structure in the same company in both the public and private market spaces. This ability to invest in a cross-asset manner has allowed GIC's active strategies to identify and participate in investment opportunities that would otherwise not be accessible.

5. *Global presence—skilled and experienced talent pool.* GIC is a global investment organization with 10 offices located worldwide, staffed by skilled and experienced investment and business professionals. This combination of a global presence and deep expertise allows GIC to be close to key financial markets worldwide, with "boots on the ground" to identify investment opportunities and build relationships with key stakeholders across the world.

6.6. CONCLUSION

Investing is inherently a risky business. In addition, we believe that the world will increasingly be characterized by volatility and uncertainty. Against this backdrop, investing in a diversified manner over the long term within a robust risk management framework and clear governance structure remains the most prudent approach for a large, global, long-term investor like GIC.

7. MANAGER INTERVIEW: DENNIS STATTMAN, CFA

Larry Cao, CFA

Dennis Stattman, CFA, is an adviser to BlackRock's Multi-Asset Strategies Group. Mr. Stattman's service with the firm dates back to 1989, including his years with Merrill Lynch Investment Managers (MLIM), which merged with BlackRock in 2006. He joined Merrill Lynch Investment Managers as a portfolio manager of the Merrill Lynch Global Allocation Fund at the Fund's inception in 1989. Mr. Stattman served as a portfolio manager of the Global Allocation Fund/s until his retirement. He previously served as a member of BlackRock's Global Operating and Leadership Committees. From 1989 through 1996, he was also a portfolio manager of the Merrill Lynch Special Value Fund. Prior to joining MLIM, Mr. Stattman served as the director of research for Meridian Management Company and as a pension investment officer for the World Bank, supervising the management of US equities in the Bank's Retirement Plan. He holds a BS degree in commerce from the University of Virginia and an MBA degree, with honors, from the University of Chicago.

7.1. THE BEGINNING

Larry Cao, CFA, CFA Institute: I first came across your fund when I was managing similar products. We had a team that just focused on asset allocation and manager selection. Then each of the selected managers, with their deep resources, managed a slice of the fund. Your team managed the entire process and yet your fund has always stood its own. How did you come up with the idea?

Dennis Stattman, CFA: The idea originated in a synthesis that occurred in a meeting back in 1988 at Merrill Lynch Asset Management. The people in the meeting were my former investment partner Bryan Ison; Norman Harvey, the equity funds investment officer, who was my first boss at Merrill Lynch Asset Management; and Arthur Zeikel, the head of Merrill Lynch Asset Management, who wrote the book on portfolio management that CFA course work included for many years—and me.

We began with the basic idea for a mutual fund that would try to protect clients against the sort of shock (and loss of principal) that they suffered in the 1987 stock market crash. The first thread was a more cautious trade-off in risk and return than that embodied in most mutual funds.

The second thread also came from the 1987 stock market crash, because there was then a tell that something was going to go badly wrong—and it was that long-term interest rates shot up very rapidly immediately before the crash and ripped that theoretical, fundamental underpinning out from under equity securities pricing. But back then, investors tended to be very constrained to investing *within* asset classes, so we wanted a fund that was not only free, but encouraged, to roam across asset classes to take advantage of return opportunities or to guard against risk due to mispricing across asset classes.

The third element—and I would like to think that I was mostly responsible for this—was that we took a global orientation. At the time, there was something called international investing and it was considered cutting edge. I had the good fortune from 1980 to 1984 to work for the pension fund of the World Bank in Washington, DC. There, we were very globally oriented. We also did a lot of asset allocation work, and that taught me the mental construct for global asset allocation.

Then there was a final piece, and this was, I think, very important and unique. My colleague Bryan Ison and I were both very committed practitioners of bottom-up security selection. That brought the unique attribute of our approach: We combined both top-down asset allocation and bottom-up security selection.

Early on, we came to be able to articulate our approach and value proposition and to do so in a limited number of words: We manage a very diversified portfolio of stocks, bonds, and cash-equivalent worldwide to deliver a competitive return with significantly less risk than an equity-only product. While that sounds pretty simple, and it is simple, it was a radical idea then.

Cao: And not easy to do at all.

Stattman: It is not easy. Ken Kroner, a former colleague here at BlackRock, and I once did an interview on global multi-asset investing for an internal publication. The interviewer paused at some point and said, this way of investing makes so much sense, why doesn't everybody do that? Then there was kind of a moment of silence and Ken said, "Well, because it's hard!"

The truth is, in many ways, it is hard because of the very reason it is a good thing to do. There is a big opportunity set, but utilizing that opportunity set requires a lot of work and constant evolution of your tool set. You are in a competitive environment where you are touching a lot of areas in the securities market, but you have to be very careful because you are working in the context of a generalist, and many of those market areas have specialists who confine their entire working lives to them.

You must always be careful, and I have always told the team that you must play your own game. You do not want to play somebody else's game; you do not want to sit down and play a game against a player who plays it 24/7 when you just wandered in and you are a rookie. So, there is actual tension between being an effective generalist, taking advantage of the breadth of your opportunity set, and at the same time being very careful that you are not getting out beyond your capabilities in doing something that is a very specialized activity that you are the least qualified to do.

Cao: Fascinating. The story of your first meeting is fascinating. The four threads you mentioned are all among the core principles in managing a multi-asset product. And your story of how the interviewer realizes that this could be the way that everybody invests—that is really the point of our book. We want to highlight the benefits of multi-asset investing for everyone to see that this is one way, and probably the only way, that people should be investing.

7.2. THE EVOLUTION

Cao: The analytical challenge of managing such a product is tremendous. You need quantitative skills and fundamental skills. You need people who understand all kinds of different stocks and all kinds of different bonds. How were you able to put a team together? What is the division of labor between portfolio managers and analysts? Related to that, I am also curious to learn about Bryan's background.

Stattman: I guess that I should start by saying that the hardest thing that ever happened in my career is that Bryan took disability retirement in 2002. Fortunately, by then, we had built a team. We had 12–14 people at that time, and some very experienced analysts stepped up and took much more responsibility. That helped a lot, but it was personally and professionally difficult for all of us. I still talk with Bryan about the markets. He is just not formally part of the team.

We have always been collaborators, and back when we started Global Allocation, we worked with four other portfolio management groups: a cash management group that did all our short-term stuff, a fixed-income group that did the security selection for the fixed-income part, a European security selection team, and a Pacific Basin security selection team. The European and the Pacific teams picked only stocks. Over time we took these "in house." The first part that we took in house was fixed income. And it took us several years or so to begin to fully take in the European and Pacific-Basin stock selection.

Cao: Can you elaborate on how you took over the fixed-income investments?

Stattman: There were two portfolio managers that headed it up back then, and they had the analytical and currency capabilities. We pretty quickly decided that we could do it better ourselves, and we just did it ourselves. Bryan Ison did most of it.

It was pretty simple stuff until 1990, when the junk bond market blew up. At that time, there were regulatory changes that forced insurance companies and savings and loans to divest a lot of junk bonds, and there was a huge dislocation because they were essentially forced to sell.

We were able to start buying junk bonds, and we just looked at them the way we looked at stocks. We used our equity capability. Back then, it was just the three of us: Bryan Ison, Steve Cohen, and me. We added our first analyst, Karen Morley, in 1991. That is when we started to build the team.

Cao: And what tools did you have access to?

Stattman: The tools we use have evolved enormously over time, just as the environment and technological toolkit have evolved over time. Back in 1989, it was a different world. When I came to work for Merrill Lynch Asset Management in 1989, I brought my own computer because having a computer on your desk was not normal.

Cao: Was your computer a 386 back in those days?

Stattman: Exactly, it was a pretty primitive thing. Our original portfolio information system was an Excel spreadsheet that we created ourselves.

Of the original three people on the team, two also worked on another product. We started with US$129 million in one fund. Today, we are $78 billion in 11 products. With a small exception, all of the products do the same thing but in different regulatory wrappers. We evolved to what is now a 56+ dedicated person team, all working on Global Allocation. We think about the portfolio holistically both from a bottom-up and top-down perspective, as opposed to a "fund of funds" approach. I think we have the best tool set in the industry, including the best multi-asset risk analysis capabilities, given BlackRock's vast resources.

Cao: It would be very interesting to go over how your capabilities evolved together with the industry.

Stattman: I will just touch on what I think were three of the stages. The first was what I call the dark ages, which lasted up until the late 90s. The dark ages meant it was totally do-it-ourselves. I feel like we did a pretty good job most of the time, but it was primitive. The second I would call Merrill Lynch risk analysis capabilities. That is where we started getting some help from the firm itself, but I will say that, compared to anything we have today at BlackRock, it was quite rudimentary. Then the third stage I will call BlackRock RQA (Risk and Quantitative Analysis), BlackRock's corporate risk analysis. That is how we have evolved.

Let me hasten to add that this is a very dynamic situation. The tools that BlackRock provides us and the interaction that we have with RQA are constantly evolving. We make use of both the off-the-shelf capabilities that BlackRock has designed and also continuous ad hoc risk analyses for the questions that we need to answer on a current basis.

BlackRock offers very powerful risk analysis. What is more, BlackRock developed its own multi-asset risk engine. Most of what passes as risk analysis in our industry is actually based upon someone else's risk analysis engines that were typically developed for either stocks or bonds, but they were not from a multi-asset foundation.

Cao: The lack of multi-asset risk analytic tools is a very important point.

7.3. THE PROCESS

Cao: You said that you want to be free to roam around across different asset classes. How free are you? Has it changed over time?

Stattman: We are very free. The way to think of our limitation is that our original wrapper is a 1940 Act mutual fund. We have the regulation that comes along with that. But our real limitation is twofold, and these are perfectly acceptable; we can live with them. Number one, we only invest in securities except for very, very limited exceptions. We do not buy brick-and-mortar real estate; we can buy a REIT, but not the underlying physical asset. The other limitation is that we do not use leverage. In other words, we do not borrow money or use derivatives in a way that would effectively make us more than 100% invested. I will add one limitation: We must be able to price everything that we hold in the portfolio daily because we are a daily opening mutual fund. In other words, people can buy or sell our mutual fund on any day that the New York Stock Exchange is open, and so we must have a pricing mechanism for every investment in the portfolio. Those are the walls that we work within, but it surely gives us a lot of investment choices.

Cao: How did you determine the size of the individual bets? It has something to do with how you reconcile your top-down convictions with your bottom-up security selection.

Stattman: This is a really great question. And it goes precisely to an important point, in that our approach has evolved enormously over time. Let me hasten to tell you, back in the 90s, this was a very rudimentary exercise of comparing our asset mix, currency mix, and country weightings against our benchmark and reviewing our security weightings in absolute terms.

It has always been the case that we have avoided making great big bets on any individual security. Probably the biggest weighting we ever had in any equity security was a little over 2%. That was a stock that we regarded as a unique opportunity and pretty safe. Today, the considerations that go into our weightings are both quantitative and qualitative, as always. But the quantitative side of our capability has evolved very far. Effectively, the toolkit available to us is much bigger than it was even a few years ago.

The way we implement weightings has evolved a great deal. Today we have a part of the team called the PCC, Portfolio Construction Center, that is responsible for pulling together all the information for us to design and implement what we think is the most efficient use of our risk budget. The PCC also determines how we can most efficiently transact in the market, and we are talking about big money here.

Cao: It is impossible to move some of these portfolios around, I am sure.

Stattman: With $78 billion, moving 1% of the portfolio from this to that implies over $1.5 billion of transactions. You really have to know what you are doing to accomplish that without disrupting the market. And there are smart ways to do things—efficient, inexpensive ways.

So, let us say that we are going to increase our US stock exposure. We could buy individual stocks, or we could buy a basket. That basket could be targeted to the overall market, or it could be targeted to a subset of the market: a sectoral subset, a factor subset, a geographic subset, or some combination of the above. We could buy futures contracts. We could initiate an option transaction or an option spread transaction. For that matter, it could be a total return swap. We do not do a lot of those, but I am just giving you a sense of the menu of possibilities that we think about every time we go about making a change in the portfolio. The analysis of how best to do that is conducted by our Portfolio Construction Center. The decision making lies with our portfolio managers, but they are informed and supported by that Portfolio Construction Center.

Cao: We are big believers of that too, because the CFA Program is really training someone to be a part of a multi-asset team. We are really training people in all the relevant skills.

Can you elaborate on your risk budget?

Stattman: Back when we started, we did not even know what the term risk budget meant. We kind of had one in our heads, and it was "how different from the benchmark can we be?" The answer was "a whole lot different." Can a particular difference really blow us up, and under what kind of circumstances in the world will it blow us up? How far can we push our view of the world? At one point, we held only half our benchmark weighting in stocks and, at a different time, half our benchmark weighting in bonds. Our benchmark is 60% US dollars, but at our maximum, we were about 93% US dollars. We had huge bets versus the benchmark. When we first started, we had 200 securities in the portfolio, tops. We typically have 700+ now.

So, now the risk budget is a concept that we use a lot. We use it in a fashion where our drawdowns versus the equity market tend to be small. Part of the reason for that is that we are value investors. Also, in times past, we could often find fixed-income securities—whether high-yield bonds or emerging market bonds—that would give us equity-like returns, but with much less risk. Those days are gone, at least for now, by the way.

I should hasten to add, we are always looking for where the opportunity is and our portfolio managers, our analysts, have always been multi-asset. They have always been encouraged to look wherever in the capital structure, the best risk–reward trade-off is.

Cao: When you adjust your portfolios, do you do it at a regular interval or when opportunities arise? If it is bottom-up, how much does the top-down perspective come into the decision?

Stattman: We have the ability to make changes to our model portfolio daily, but they are typically small, incremental changes. They are mostly bottom-up. We meet formally at minimum once a week to look at the top-down portfolio, but practically speaking, it is a continuous conversation.

The top-down changes tend to be somewhere between 10 bps to 100 bps of the portfolio. The changes are then communicated to our Portfolio Construction Center with some ideas of how the portfolio managers think they should be implemented. The PCC will evaluate that and let us know what *they* think will be the best way to implement the change and whether there could be any kind of unanticipated portfolio impacts. Typically, portfolio changes are completed in about 1–3 days.

Cao: When you think about unintended bets or tactical top-down decisions, what is the reference? If it is all bottom-up, what is the reference that you look at from a top-down perspective?

Stattman: We look at two things. We have a reference benchmark that is 36% US stocks, 24% non-US stocks, 24% US fixed income, and 16% non-US fixed income. The way we came up with that benchmark was way back at the inception of the fund, the four of us said "We want a global fund whose risk level is consistent with a benchmark that is 60% stock and 40% fixed income. We will largely have US dollar–based clients, so we will make it 60% US and 40% non-US."

Cao: One thing your fund does that many similar funds do not do is currency. Can you also give us some examples when forex hedging worked or did not work?

Stattman: We think that foreign exchange (FX) is an area that from time to time presents an important opportunity. We have varied our currency exposure from perhaps as low as 40% USD to as high as 93% USD, and the way we think about it is in value terms.

Our clients look at us as a US dollar–denominated fund. There were times that the dollar was very attractive, other times unattractive. We went through a period of time before the financial crisis where we saw the dollar was quite unattractive. We were seriously underweight, and it helped our client returns a great deal. Later, we came to fundamental conclusions about the changes in relative monetary policies and national economic performance that, along with the level of the dollar, led us to a significant dollar overweight. By the way, this involves a lot of decision making and trading that is difficult and time consuming.

Cao: It is. Some people think it might be even tougher than stock or bond selection.

Stattman: It can seem that way. But if you realize that we are not trying to capture every single foreign currency move, but rather, we just want to be generally on the right side of the long-term moves, it a bit easier. Knowing whether the Japanese yen (JPY) is going to be at 112 or 120 is hard, but for example, knowing that the Bank of Japan does not want the yen to be strong, sometimes that is not so hard.

Cao: Your fund also has the capability to go short. Can you also give us some examples where short selling has worked or not worked for you?

Stattman: One can put shorting in two different categories. One of them is simple index-level hedging, and that is not what we really mean by short selling. What we mean would be shorting individual securities. We can have 20% of the total net assets of the portfolio net short in individual securities. We use this shorting capability on a limited basis. We used it immediately prior to and during the financial crisis. It really helped on the way down. When things started to come back, we eliminated shorting individual stocks for a long time.

Over the past year or year and a half, we asked the team to focus more on finding short candidates because we believe sometime, and we do not know exactly when this is going to be, there will be a day of reckoning for valuation in the US stock market. The US stock market is priced at about 26 times cyclically adjusted P/E. Those valuation levels historically have shown themselves to be poor entry points for very long-term investors, and we are very long-term investors.

But cyclically adjusted P/E is not a good short-to-intermediate-term timing tool, and so what we try to do is to find individual securities to short that we think are unattractive for purchase from a risk–reward point of view and where the fundamentals are deteriorating and use them as both individual shorts and also to hedge our longs. I lived through the tech bubble; I lived through the mortgage finance bubble; and so, I developed a pretty keen appreciation that when the stock market gets into silly season, there is no telling how silly it is going to get. All you had to do was to live through 1999 to understand that. The US stock market is in silly season now, and I do not want us to get killed on the short side while people are still kind of going crazy on the upside. But I think you will see us use our short capability more in the coming year or two.

7.4. THE WAR STORIES

Cao: What type of asset classes were you investing into? And how has that grown over time?

Stattman: The most important insight that has helped us, over time, came from my former partner, Bryan Ison. Bryan said "an asset class is whatever you decide it is." For 20 years, the industry's idea of asset classes amounted to only stocks, bonds, or cash, and the real opportunity for us has been one layer below that surface view—in the sub-asset-classes because those are the areas that tend to get mispriced and to offer either an unusually good or bad return per unit of risk.

I will mention three examples: (1) the Japanese equity market; (2) junk bonds; and (3) US bank stocks, which suffered a tremendous dislocation in the 1989–1990 bear market and offered a tremendous opportunity.

The big question when we started Global Allocation was what to do about the Japanese stock market. And that is hard to imagine now because most people cannot understand that in early 1989, Japanese equities were the biggest capitalization market in the world and were also dramatically overvalued. However, they had been overvalued for at least half a decade, and any number of practitioners had ruined their careers betting against the Japanese stock market in the 1980s. So there we were, it was a big chunk of our benchmark, and we had to figure out what to do. We are value investors; what in the world should we do about the Japanese stock market? Now, you asked how big the negative bet on Japan was. I think we were about half the weighting of the Japanese equity market.

This is a moment to add one additional element. Security selection was also very important. We were fortunate to work with a fabulous team, which at the time was the Merrill Lynch Pacific Fund team, headed by Steve Silverman. Steve has a really good record. He sat about a hundred feet away from us. We would talk everyday about the Japanese stock market, particular stocks, and his team ran a concentrated portfolio for us that was very risk aware. For example, a big chunk of our portfolio was in deeply undervalued Japanese non-life insurance companies that had large securities portfolios trading at a big discount to net asset value plus good underwriting businesses. They were a way of owning the Japanese stock market with lower risk and good valuation.

The third protective measure that we took was buying puts, so that when the market came apart in late 1989 and early 1990, we had some hedges in place. So, we effectively had no exposure to the part of the Japanese stock market that blew up.

It was that threefold approach that I think illustrates the strengths of the Global Allocation team. While we implemented top-down underweighting, we also had bottom-up securities selection that made our Japanese stocks much different from the Japanese stock market and also used derivatives to achieve a different risk–reward trade-off for our portfolio than you could get simply with an index or portfolio of securities. I am proud to tell you that was way back 28 years ago.

The Japanese stock market was an example of something to avoid. The high-yield bond market and US bank stock sectors were examples for sub-asset-classes that offered disproportionately high return-to-risk trade-offs. Focusing on sub-asset-classes has illuminated not only our top-down work but has also helped guide where we apply resources in bottom-up security selection.

A key facet of our competitive advantage has always been this bottom-up capability, and it does two things for us. First, it allows one to find individual securities that may outperform the market. Second, it forces you to validate or check your top-down ideas with how the situation really looks on the ground. So, if you see a national equity market that looks attractive, when you try to find individual securities in that market, you may discover that that there is something odd in that market. Perhaps it is deeply skewed to one particular sector or risk. When you look under the averages, do you find that things are not really so attractive or do you find "wow, there are a whole group of very interesting securities here?" So, we did not come up with the US bank stock sector as an idea purely top-down and just bought a basket.

Instead, we had the idea because we not only see things top-down, but we dug in, looked at individual stocks, talked to managements, came up with opinions about what the loan losses were likely to be compared with reserves. We could be confident that the opportunities were there not just on some sort of valuation or situational basis but also on a stock-by-stock set of opportunities—an extraordinarily rich and unusual opportunity.

Cao: Let us summarize, and maybe then you can give us some highlights on what you think made BlackRock Global Allocation the fund it is today.

Stattman: The most important thing is focusing on doing a good job for clients by delivering a consistent outcome—a competitive return with less risk than the typical equity fund. We have been consistent. Our benchmark may sound sort of old fashioned, but we have not changed it since we started because we want to be consistent and predictable. We want a broad range of clients to be able to have global diversification and a portfolio return that will allow to them to reach their return objectives *and* sleep at night. It is simple in its appeal, and we aim to do it over and over again. Of course, the way we do it evolves over time with technology and with the markets. I feel that we have done a good job.

Cao: That is backed up by your long-term performance. And I would also say the 40% non-US allocation was very aggressive back then.

Stattman: I am very grateful to two organizations for helping me build my professional foundation. I want to mention Merrill Lynch Asset Management for being a leader in what we used to call international investing and to see that approach was just a step on the road to the real idea, which is global investing. All investing is global. We were fortunate from the beginning of Global Allocation Fund to have the freedom to roam the world's markets, while most managers were—and many still are—constrained to much narrower mandates.

Also, I was very lucky to work at the World Bank and to have great colleagues at the pension fund that taught me how to think globally. It was a fabulous way to start my career after business school and showed me an industry perspective that I would never have obtained in any other way. I was given the ability to meet with the smartest people in the investment business and the opportunity to have regular asset allocation conversations in a worldwide context. That job was a godsend.

Building on that foundation, I was fortunate to have the opportunity to work at the largest asset manager in the world, with access to cutting-edge technology and risk management tools. BlackRock has done a tremendous job on that front. And finally, for me it has been particularly rewarding to work with a great team of intellectually curious people with a "go anywhere" mandate, such as Global Allocation, and have the freedom to invest across assets, regions, sectors, securities, and currencies.

8. MANAGER INTERVIEW: BEN INKER, CFA

Larry Cao, CFA

Ben Inker, CFA, is head of GMO's Asset Allocation team and a member of the GMO board of directors. He joined GMO in 1992 following the completion of his BA in economics from Yale University. In his years at GMO, Mr. Inker has served as an analyst for the Quantitative Equity and Asset Allocation teams, as a portfolio manager of several equity and asset allocation portfolios, as co-head of the International Quantitative Equities and Developed Fixed-Income teams, and as CIO of Quantitative Developed Equities.

8.1. ASSET ALLOCATION: THE GMO PHILOSOPHY AND PROCESS

Larry Cao, CFA, CFA Institute: What asset classes does your team invest in, and what criteria does the team use to make these decisions?

Ben Inker, CFA: In principle, we invest in liquid financial assets of all kinds, leaving illiquid assets such as private lending, venture capital, or real estate off the table. In practice, we focus on areas like equity, credit, and alternative assets that we think we know how to analyze. The key criteria are whether this is an area where we understand where the returns come from and that we are comfortable with how we would go about determining if we are being adequately paid for the risks involved. The other is whether we can understand the risks involved. If we have these things, it is on the table.

Cao: When you say risk, do you mean that you have a history where you can analyze the volatility, etc.?

Inker: We are less focused on questions such as, "Do I have enough history to calculate a decent covariance matrix?" A real advantage of running an unlevered portfolio is you can afford to worry about only the kind of event that will lead to a permanent impairment of capital, such as the risk of depression, significant unanticipated inflation, or massive physical destruction of property in a war or natural disaster.

The other thing we think that can lead to a permanent impairment of capital has to do with pricing. If you pay too much for an asset and that asset price comes down, you will lose money that you have no expectation will come back.

Cao: When you do asset allocation, what type of things do you look at? Can you walk us through the basic process?

Inker: When we are looking at an asset class or strategy, the first thing we do is ask what risk an asset owner is bearing. Or, what risk does this strategy open you up to? There are certain kinds of risk we think you can and should be compensated for over time. The more depression risk is embodied in an asset, for example, the more you should be paid.

Equities do badly in a depression, which is why there is a decent equity risk premium. Our process within equities tends to be reasonably simple: As the first approximation, they will all do badly in a depression. Do not assume there should be a strongly differentiated performance in equities on the basis that some of them are deemed less risky than others.

We then ask the question, how is that return generated? And what valuations or characteristics are consistent with earning that return?

We start with the presumption that equities earn a return that is driven by the cash flows available to shareholders, and when we are thinking about a broad group of stocks, the safest assumption to make is that they will earn a return on capital that is equivalent to their cost of capital.

Our standard process starts by saying we think equities should give a risk premium of about 3% over government bonds and 4% over cash; if cash is to give 1.5% real, equities should give 5.5% or 6% real. So, we want to get inflation plus 5.5% to 6% out of equities, and the way we think you can get that out of equities is if the normalized earnings yield for equities is at least that.

If the stock market is trading at about 16 times normalized earnings, we are going to say, "Great, it's priced to deliver 5.5% to 6% real." If the P/E is lower than that, it is cheap and it is going to have a higher expected rate of return. And if it is higher than that, it is expensive and it is going to have a lower expected rate of return.

Cao: So the P/E, does it have a time series or is it just kind of something you feel is fairly stable over time?

Inker: The two circumstances where the fair P/E should change is either because the equity risk premium has changed in a general way, or the underlying return to the less risky assets has changed.

In recent years, we have been grappling with the question, Has the underlying return to cash and bonds fallen permanently? Today's yields are significantly lower than history. The question is, Are they going to rise to historically normal levels or not? It would be convenient to know whether they will because equities are a very long-duration asset. It is not enough to say cash rates are low today, and therefore, the fair P/E is high. If the cash rate is going to be higher five years from now, the vast majority of the value you will have gotten from stocks is still to come and should be discounted back at that higher rate. Stocks are worth more if there has been a permanent shift lower in interest rates, but a temporary shift, even for a reasonably long time, is much less important. With regard to whether the normal P/E changes, it might. To me, the most likely reason why it might have changed is if the underlying return to cash and bonds has fallen.

Cao: The process is systematic in the sense that you are applying the same philosophy. But it seems more fundamental than quantitative?

Inker: What we try to do is to not necessarily put together a regression model on the explanatory variables. We do the best job we can to explain what returns are and what they were. Fundamentally, what are the ways these returns are generated, and can we come up with decent estimates of what they will be?

Jeremy Grantham's background was as a fundamental stock picker. When he was putting together his estimates on what the fair value was for the stocks, he broke it down into pieces that he could understand. So, when he was looking at broader asset classes, that was his preferred way of doing things. I have spent 25 years working with the guy, and I have been brainwashed.

One of the nice things about starting with thinking about the fundamentals is that it gives you the ability to look at new assets and yet have a framework that works. Another plus is that it helps you maintain confidence in a viewpoint when the market is going the other way. If you have a model that is based on a regression of what had been working and suddenly there is a different set of things working, it would be impossible to generate continued confidence in that old set of factors.

For us, if a market that we thought was priced cheaply and should have done well turns out to do badly, we know what analysis to do and ask whether we were fundamentally wrong or is it now a better buy than it was. Frankly, to me, the greatest strength of this fundamental approach is the ability to know what questions to ask when things go wrong.

The advantage of the more heavily quantitative, rocket science approach is that if a relationship exhibits both meaningful change over a long period and is reasonably persistent over a short period, a computer can do clever things that a human being simply cannot. There are also situations where you can potentially do something very cool by taking advantage of the correlation between assets that have meaningfully different expected returns. You could do something like recognize if a currency is showing a relatively high beta and, at the same time, is expensive and therefore has a lower expected return, whereas equities are decently priced and therefore good for the risk premium. You can own the stocks, short that currency, and you have taken out the risk and kept a lot of return. That is the kind of thing that is better done by a fully quantitative system that can juggle many things at once.

Cao: I think the fundamental story is probably the easiest story to tell to investors.

Inker: Frankly, the ability to tell the story to investors in a way that they can understand is important because one of the things about making asset class-level decisions is that we do suffer somewhat from a lack of breadth. There are not that many asset classes to choose from in the end, so your odds of looking wrong over a given time period are fairly high. In our view, you need to be willing to give a multi-asset manager a good deal of time to prove whether they are doing a good job for you or not.

Cao: Can you give us some examples of how you apply the process to analyzing different types of strategies?

Inker: We want to try to come to a fundamental understanding of what risk we are underwriting. If we take a carry strategy in currencies, we can look at the historic relationships and note that one of the things that seems to have been true is that carry strategies have positive stock market beta.

High interest rate currencies in general tend to be from countries that require external financing and tend to be somewhat riskier. They are subject to the risk of those global capital flows. The reality is that this is a permanent source of risk for carry. There should be a return to that. The key second step for us is that our asset class forecast embodies what we think the current payment for risk in this asset is relative to a sustainable level.

Life gets a little bit more complicated when we are dealing with strategies that are more dynamic. A strategy that we are allocating to today is merger arbitrage, which does not really look like it has a lot of beta. But can you imagine scenarios in which many of these deals go bad at the same time? The most obvious scenarios would be a depression, an economic disaster, or a marketplace disaster, a situation in which the financial markets have seized up. So, we would argue a big part of the reason why you get paid to do merger arbitrage is because it is giving you many of the same risks as stocks. The beta looks low under normal circumstances, but it is not the normal circumstances that matter.

Cao: I recall listening to Jeremy Grantham speaking at the 2004 Financial Analysts Seminar. One thing he talked about was investing in timber.

Inker: Timber is a very illiquid asset class, and we do not allocate to it within our asset allocation portfolios because we think the appropriate way to get exposure to timber is to buy a forest. It is hard to make a direct comparison: Should I buy the S&P, or should I buy a forest? If you buy a forest, you will be stuck with it for a very long time.

Cao: That makes sense, so it's not as liquid as other assets you are talking about.

Inker: Yes. One of the charms of timber as commodities go is that it is relatively straightforward to understand where the returns come from. Most of the return historically from owning timberland has come from the biological growth of the trees. That is something knowable, whereas in an investment in oil futures, there are a lot of moving pieces that are fundamentally unknowable. So, I would say the reason why timber became special for us in the commodity world is that it is something that we can forecast.

Cao: On that point, how about gold? What is the source of return for gold?

Inker: I will admit I do not know. As a general rule, we have not allocated to gold.

Gold is weird even as commodities go. Oil is fundamentally an economic commodity. As the price goes up, we find ways to do with less; when the price goes down, we tend to use more. Gold is not consumed. If the price of gold were to go up tenfold or fall 90%, there are no obvious consequences for the global economy. And that to me makes it very difficult to try to answer the question, Is gold a good buy or a bad buy at today's price?

8.2. PERFORMANCE EVALUATION

Cao: What would be an appropriate way to measure your success? When clients come to you to buy in one of these strategies, what are the things they are looking for?

Inker: If we start with the portfolio with an agreed-upon benchmark, our job is of course to beat that benchmark over a market cycle.

The dream would be for you to have a manager outperform by taking less risk. In the absence of that, I think the manager can help by outperforming at the normal risk level or performing similarly to the benchmark with significantly lower risk. Both outcomes are improving the risk/reward trade-offs of your portfolios.

Sometimes stocks are priced to deliver a lower rate of return than bonds. There are other times—and from my standpoint, today is one of them—where the expected return premium of stocks over bonds is lower than normal, but it is still positive. That makes it harder to add that much value to a stock/bond decision because we are not actually going to make money from that decision. Overweighting stocks makes no sense today, but if we move money from stocks to bonds, we are decreasing the expected return of our portfolio.

Decisions within risk groups, in particular within riskier assets, are somewhat easier. I do not think it is cheating if we wind up overweight US equities relative to international equities during the course of a cycle. They are both equities and have similar levels of risks. If we are making such a bet consistently, I hope we are adding value, but we are not systematically being untrue to the spirit of the benchmark.

Cao: Asset allocation should be part of the multi-asset manager's toolkits though, right?

Inker: Yes. Moving money between stocks and bonds can improve the portfolio risk/reward trade-off over time. But over any given period, asset allocation can be a plus or a minus. I do not expect that we will add value from the stock/bond decision in every five-year period, but given a long period, I believe we will.

Cao: So, you are basically putting in a constraint to your strategy that "I don't deviate that much."

Inker: I am happy to deviate when stocks are cheaper than normal or stocks are more expensive than normal. What I do not want to do is deviate and say, "Look! Stocks deliver 6, bonds deliver 3. My benchmark is two-thirds stocks, one-third bonds. An obvious way I can get a return higher than that is by being four-fifth stocks, one-fifth bonds." Being systematically overweight stocks versus your client's benchmark to capture the long-run positive equity risk premium is cheating in my book.

Cao: Not necessarily, right, when things go wrong, the bear cycle can go and last for a bit of time?

Inker: If that is true, you will have underperformed if you overweight stocks. Bear markets are, of course, inevitable. If there were no bear markets, there would be no reason for an equity risk premium in the first place. But given that bear markets exist and an equity risk premium exists, owning more equities should increase the expected return of the portfolio in the long run. That does not mean systematically owning extra equities is necessarily a good idea, though.

To me, at the end of the day, if the clients thought 65:35 was an appropriate benchmark, it is because they thought that is generally an appropriate risk level. They could have signed up for 80:20. If the client likes the risk characteristics of a 65:35 portfolio and you "outperform" by giving them an 80:20 portfolio on average, you probably have not actually helped them in the end.

Cao: In this sense, the benchmark-free kind of fund is easier to do, considering the return and the risk?

Inker: To me, the charm of the benchmark-free investing style and the reason why we really like that name is that if we are freed of the necessity of worrying about our tracking error, we can put together a portfolio that has a better expected return with lower risk, because we aren't wasting any assets buying overvalued asset classes for fear that they might go up more.

The biggest distinction is not so much that it is intrinsically better to manage without the benchmark, but that we should be able to deliver a better absolute risk/reward trade-off if the only thing that we are concerned about is absolute risk and absolute return.

We got into the benchmark-free style of investing because of our experience in 1999. US equities were expensive and represented about 50% of the overall benchmark. At the time, we had only 25% of our multi-asset portfolio invested in US equities. This was almost certainly not the right answer for clients concerned about tracking error as we had a 25-point bet. Almost nothing else in the portfolio mattered except for that bet.

For clients who were concerned about absolute risk and absolute return, we had 25% of the portfolio in an asset class we thought would deliver negative real returns for the next 10 years. We had no good reason to own any US equities from an absolute risk and return perspective. The only reason to own them was a concern about our tracking error to the benchmark.

One reality is, even though we have a fund that specifically calls itself Benchmark-Free Allocation Fund, I think it's appropriate to ask the question as to whether we have outperformed the passive alternative in the long run. It is unavoidable to be asking the question, How have we done versus our competitive universe?

8.3. HOW THE GMO TEAM ADDS VALUE

RISK-FACTOR-DRIVEN ALLOCATION

Cao: Moving from benchmarking to how you add value, what are the major contributors and how much do you expect from the contributors?

Inker: Over the course of a market cycle, we expect overall tracking error of our benchmark-sensitive portfolios to be about 4%–5%. Although I would say over time maybe it's a 50:50 split between security selection and asset allocation, the amount of tracking error I want to take on over the course of a cycle is going to vary quite widely depending on the opportunities we see.

Cao: How do you think about risk and build portfolios?

Inker: We tend to like to break down an asset from a risk perspective into a few risk factors we care about. For example:

- Depression risk: Here we are trying to quantify how bad we think things would be for our strategies during a depression.
- Inflation risk: In an unanticipated inflation of certain severity, how bad are things going to be?
- Liquidity risk: We know about liquidity shock; how much do we think prices would be hit?

We don't have many factors. When putting together the portfolios, it's about asking the question, How much do I get paid today when taking depression risk? The more we are paid, the more risk we are willing to take.

The reality, though, is that it's exceptionally hard to find an asset that simply embodies depression risk and nothing else. Even if we could, it's still hard to try to figure out what we are getting paid today for owning it.

We are going to buy assets, or potentially strategies, that embody a package of risks. Although we want to look at risks in a factor sense, we really want to look at returns in an asset sense. We can value an asset, but it's harder to value liquidity or another theoretical factor.

Risk is inherently a multi-factor concept. Maybe we are getting paid a lot to take liquidity risk in emerging debt, and very little in small-cap stocks. If that's true, we don't want to have a single liquidity factor where we are saying we want to be long liquidity risk, but we want to focus on understanding the risks we care about and where we can get paid decently for taking them.

Cao: Can you contrast the GMO approach with risk parity?

Inker: We are not just asking the question, If we look at this global equity factor, how much are we being paid? The risk is closer to the generic risk factor, but the return is embedded in the assets we own. That for us is kind of the important twist.

One of the things we worry about when people go too far down the route to factor investing (e.g., risk parity) is the presumption that relationships remain constant, which is effectively assuming the risk premium into existence.

If we say bonds have a term premium, then that term premium is a payment for unanticipated inflation risk. So, in the risk parity portfolio, we would want to have as much risk on term premium as we do on equity premium. We will be 30% stocks, 70% bonds, and levered up to a standard amount. One of the things that worries us is levering up, because now we have created financing risk and that was a risk that did not exist otherwise.

The other worry is that, historically, we can all agree bonds have outperformed cash; and a possible reason for this is that you are taking inflation risk and it's possibly embodied in your assets. But let's say right now, the yield curve is flat. If you are sitting in Japan, how certain are you of the term premium there? The way we see bonds and cash in the US, it is not clear whether there is a risk premium for bonds today. But it's easier to make the case in Japan or, frankly, in the UK, that the risk premium for bonds is zero or negative. The concern we have is really about a presumption that a risk premium will be there even if you cannot point to the sources of return right now such that today's price will give it to you.

The magic of risk parity in recent years has frankly been that stocks and bonds have been negatively correlated. So, the risk parity portfolio has a wonderful advantage in that you have reduced volatility. With a negative correlation, if you run stocks and bonds together at similar volatility levels, the portfolio will have lower volatility overall. That isn't always the case. If you are running it with leverage and the correlation you are assuming to be negative is positive, that can be very bad for your portfolio.

Cao: What about global macro strategies?

Inker: Global macro is a complicated combination of different sources of strategies, everything from CTA to multi-factor approaches.

Most political and macroeconomic events turn out not to matter as much in the long run as they seem to in the shorter run. I would argue recessions don't matter from a whole market cycle perspective. They don't leave a big mark in the form of significantly lower aggregate earnings over a period. Earnings go down in a recession and go up in a boom, but you don't get systemic bankruptcy problems. You don't see long-term systematic losses. Depressions, on the other hand, do matter.

Global macro often means investing on the basis of your ability to predict macroeconomic events. This is a very tricky game. It is not enough to be able to predict macroeconomic events better than the other person (which is hard enough). You also have to be able to predict the market response to those events. The market response to them at some level is more behavioral than rational, because most macroeconomic events don't change the long-term fair value of assets.

If you could accurately forecast recessions, you could make some money. It's hard. If what you are really doing is forecasting a change in the market's perceived likelihood of a recession and therefore a change in the pricing of assets faster than the market can, that game is getting extra hard. I am not saying it can't be done, but it's not as simple as it first appears.

Cao: You guys might be coming from a different background with a different edge.

Inker: Yes, certainly what we do is hard in several ways. The most important edge is discipline: We stick with what we are doing and that is hard emotionally and it's a tough way to run a business.

Cao: GMO might be the most famous for sticking to your guns. The momentum strategy is always easier to run in a way: You tend to be right more of the time, and your clients are unhappy with you less often.

Inker: When you look at the performance of momentum, it has worked for stock selection because stocks with good price momentum have been more likely than average to exhibit positive earnings surprise.

The reason momentum works might be because human beings underreact. An issue with this is that if it is underreaction, it is easy to imagine that a sufficient combination of positive surprises could eventually lead to overreaction. At that point, selling at the right time would be critical.

There is evidence that momentum works in asset classes as well. We have a group within GMO that does asset allocation in a very quantitative way. By doing that, they are able to harness momentum. It's tougher for us, from a more fundamental or a judgmental approach. We don't know how to get that confidence in a momentum approach.

Cao: Are people born to be value managers or momentum managers? Switching seems really hard. The challenge with value though is when do you get to the full position?

Inker: In principle, as soon as, say, one group of stocks has a slightly higher expected rate of return than the other group of stocks, you can make the case to switch and own as much of that group of stocks as your risk budget will allow.

The problem with this approach is twofold. One is ether your tracking error is too high for your information ratio, or the absolute risks you may be taking are too high for the Sharpe ratio. The other is more behavioral: It's always comforting to be in a situation where if something you own goes down, you can buy more. That is psychologically satisfying.

In late 2008 and the beginning of 2009, we were steadily buying risk assets, but they were going down so fast that it was hard to make much headway in the overall weighting of risk assets in the portfolio.

The trade-off is between putting together a portfolio that should give a strong return in the long run versus holding out for a better entry point.

The dilemma for us was that we knew stocks were cheap in absolute terms, with forecasts that were very positive. But we were to some degree holding out with the expectation that stocks would not bottom out until they were around half of fair value. So, we kept buying, but we didn't get to the full position.

I would argue in retrospect, there was a certain amount of greed involved for us. Some of our reticence to buy risk assets in 2008–09 was about fear of a depression, but a surprising amount was about greed. It was about trying to get a better entry point.

Frankly, there is one nice thing about the framework we have for generating asset class returns. Our framework would say that in the long run, the return on capital is going to be 6%. It doesn't make sense for the market to permanently trade at a significant discount to its replacement value. When it trades cheap to replacement value, we have a high forecast. The discipline of staring at that forces us to buy. And we did buy stocks in late 2008 and early 2009; we could, though, have bought more. Our forecasts were saying this was the best opportunity to buy risk assets that we had seen within a generation.

We had thought that a good deal of the pain of the stock market falling was just an overvalued market falling to fair value. We thought it got cheap by early 2009, maybe 25% cheap to fair value. I can make an argument that at 25% cheap to fair value, you should be at your maximum weight in stocks. Sometimes you are going to have significant pain and have that 25% discount become a 50% discount, but you should make more money over time if you are prepared to get the full position of the 25% cheap. It's a hard thing to do because by the time it's 25% cheap, it would be easy to imagine you can get to 50% or even 75% below fair value.

Cao: What did it feel like in the office on those days?

Inker: We spent a lot of time focusing on the question, On the basis of history, how cheap do we think these things are going to get?

Cao: What about client withdrawals?

Inker: We had significant client withdrawals, with one reason being that our portfolios were reasonably liquid. The fact that there were outflows didn't stop us from reallocating; in some ways, it made things easier. Flows, either in or out, allow you to reallocate your portfolios kind of for free.

DYNAMIC ASSET ALLOCATION

Cao: It sounds like you don't have a specific dynamic layer. You apply your philosophy across time, and as things change, you adjust your allocation.

Inker: Yes, we don't have a dynamic long–short overlay on top of a base portfolio. We are trying to put together the right overall portfolio given the risk/reward trade-off and the price of the assets that we see.

Cao: Do you make the adjustment at a certain interval, or does it just depend on the situation?

Inker: What would cause us to change rapidly are rapid changes in price. So, the portfolio was changing more quickly in the fall of 2008 and the spring of 2009 than it did in the course of 2013 or 2014 when nothing particular was happening. But for us, it's generally three to six times a year that something meaningful enough happens to warrant a trade.

We update our asset class forecasts on a monthly basis. (We have the tools to do this on an intra-month basis, if necessary. Very seldom is it necessary.) But the fact that we get a new set of forecasts every month does not mean the target portfolio changes every month. The target portfolio changes a few times a year.

Cao: One thing we see in dynamic processes, if people do overlays of some strategies with the dynamic decision, then they end up potentially having a very high turnover. We always ask people how they make these changes and what they estimate to be the cost when making these changes, which can be significant for asset classes, such as emerging market debt.

Inker: If we are talking about something like emerging debt, it is considerable; we are buying and selling an actual portfolio of debt securities; we are not just trading a total return swap, and it could easily cost 50 bps or more in terms of roundtrip trading costs.

Cao: So, you end up making fewer of those changes because of the costs?

Inker: Yes. We are going to be somewhat cautious with an asset class like emerging market debt. But the reality is that because of the relatively slow rate of our forecast change, if it's worth buying, we'll probably be there for a couple of years; and if we are not there for that long, it's probably because we got very good returns very quickly. Let's look at the example of credit in 2016, which was a really good opportunity to buy in the winter. Credit isn't a wonderfully liquid asset class, so one hopes to be in it for a while. However, by the time we were in June or July, the spreads had come in a lot. With the yields a lot lower, it didn't make sense to hold anymore. And so we sold it, even though we had held it for only a few months. The good news is we made a couple of years' worth of returns in six months. And that's fine, too. So, we want to have reasonable thresholds between our buys and our sells in expected returns. That usually is enough to make sure that we are more than covering the transaction costs.

Cao: When you do make changes, what is the average threshold?

Inker: A trade will generally be somewhere between 2% and 10%, with trades in the higher range rare. We started the beginning of 2016 with 15% of our portfolios in TIPS. By June of 2016, we had zero, because the yield went from 55 bps to 10 bps.

TIPS are liquid, and the difference between owning TIPS and bonds and cash is a relatively less important decision. TIPS were better than nominal bonds, but the margin of superiority of the TIPS versus cash was not that big. So, moving 15% from TIPS to cash was not a profound change in the risk stance of the portfolio. Owning 15 points more of emerging market equities is quite different. First, these securities are less liquid, and they are going to take some time to buy. But, more importantly, we have just profoundly changed the risk stance of the portfolio by moving into this risky asset class. We are not likely to do that on a whim. It would take a really large change in the valuation of emerging equities to warrant a 15% shift, and that means we are very likely to make such a move in a number of steps over a significant period of time.

Cao: What challenges do you face in helping people understand your investment strategies?

Inker: We have a philosophical viewpoint that you can improve portfolios by doing dynamic asset allocations. It's also the case that the average investment committee is poorly suited to be making those decisions.

It might be slightly self-serving, but we believe you can make a traditional, fairly static portfolio better by incorporating some dynamic asset allocation. The difficulty is that it is going to take a while to see whether doing so has helped or hurt. If the manager doesn't have that much breadth, the information ratio is not going to look hugely high, even if the Sharpe ratio of the portfolio has improved. So, it's important for anyone who wants to do this to be willing to make the commitment—I am going to give this a try for a number of years. I think in order to do that the CIO or the investment committee needs to buy into the underlying philosophy to believe in what the manager is doing.

For us, we need to be dealing with people who are believers in long-term value and believers of the idea that returns are driven by the cash flows available to investors. And people who doubt those two things are going to be a bad fit.

Cao: What are your perspectives on currency hedging?

Inker: Currency can be an interesting asset, and carry is an interesting strategy that can be bought like a risk asset. With regard to currency hedging, my default would be that it's appropriate to think about bonds in currency-hedged terms, and it's appropriate to think about stocks in unhedged terms. The reason why is because the underlying cash flows of most companies are real in nature and they generate goods and services, which in many cases are unaffected by changes in real exchange rates. So, a move in the exchange rate shouldn't necessarily affect the real value of a company, and in extreme cases, the market would look right through it. The most extreme case I can think of is January 2015, when the Swiss franc broke out of its peg versus the euro. The Swiss franc appreciated versus the euro by about 15%, and in that day the stock market went down about 15%. If you held the stocks unhedged, nothing happened to the value of your portfolio. If you held Swiss stocks and hedged the currency, you lost around 30% that day with no expectation that you would ever get those losses back. That's an extreme case, but it illustrates the point. It's not that we never hedge equities. It's that if we are going to own equities, we hedge when we think there is something really interestingly mispriced about the currency.

Cao: Any final remarks for our readers?

Inker: Investing is all about risk and return, and the thing I am most appreciative about with regard to factor investing is that it makes you realize risk is not a single number. The important thing from my standpoint about the return side of investing is that you should never separate the question of where do those returns come from what the asset is priced to deliver today. If you can think intelligently about the risks that assets embody and the returns they are priced to deliver, it should work out pretty well in the end.

Made in the USA
Las Vegas, NV
03 November 2026

57422812R00102